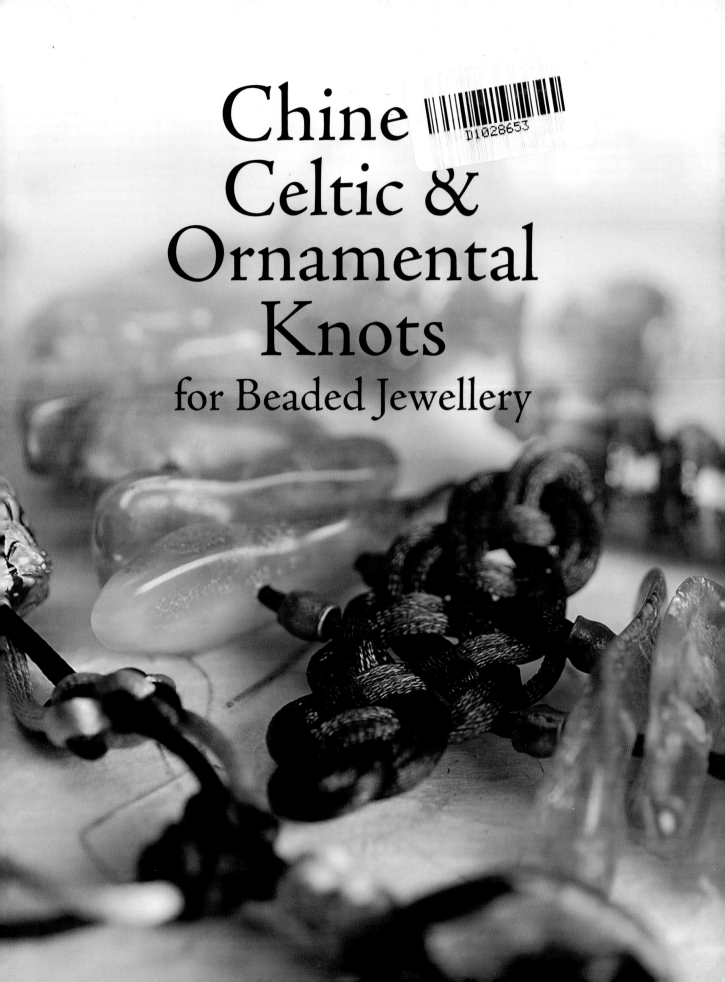

Chine
Celtic &
Ornamental
Knots
for Beaded Jewellery

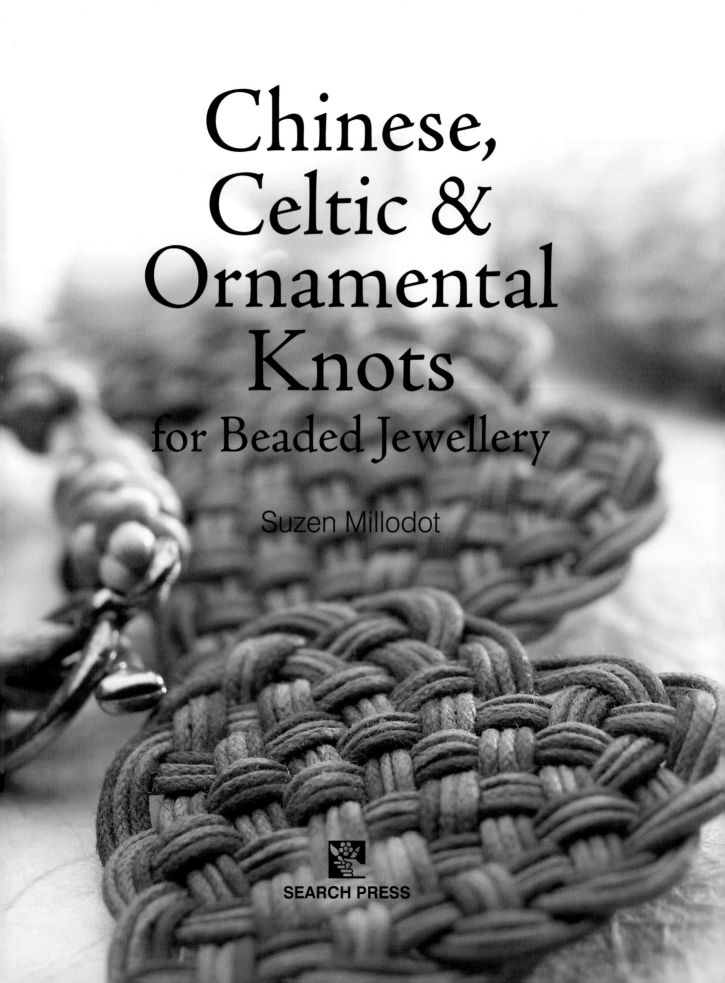

Chinese, Celtic & Ornamental Knots
for Beaded Jewellery

Suzen Millodot

SEARCH PRESS

First published in Great Britain 2012

Search Press Limited
Wellwood, North Farm Road,
Tunbridge Wells, Kent TN2 3DR

Based on the following books by Suzen Millodot, all
published by Search Press:

Chinese Knots for Beaded Jewellery (2003)
Celtic Knots for Beaded Jewellery (2005)
Ornamental Knots for Beaded Jewellery (2008)

Photographs by Debbie Patterson at Seach Press studios (pages 1–19,
132–192); Roddy Paine Photographic Studios (pages 20–131);
John Liddle, Cardiff (page 75) and Simon Hind photography (step-by-
step photography on pages 117–118).

ISBN: 978-1-84448-814-8

The Publishers and author can accept no responsibility for any
consequences arising from the information, advice or instructions given
in this publication.

Readers are permitted to reproduce any of the items in this book for
their personal use, or for the purposes of selling for charity, free of
charge and without the prior permission of the Publishers. Any use of
the items for commercial purposes is not permitted without the prior
permission of the Publishers.

Suppliers

If you have difficulty in obtaining any of the materials and equipment
mentioned in this book, then please visit the Search Press website for
details of suppliers: www.searchpress.com

You are also invited to visit the author's website:
www.ornamental-knots.com

Publisher's note

All the step-by-step photographs in this book feature the
author, Suzen Millodot, demonstrating how to tie knots
and how to make jewellery using knots. No models have
been used.

Printed in Malaysia

Contents

Materials and equipment

Cords

There is a far greater range of types of cords available now than when I started to make decorative knots, and it is much easier to find them. However, for many of us it will still be necessary to buy them by mail. One advantage of using the internet and mail order catalogues is that there is often more information available about the products on the website or in the catalogues, allowing you to plan and decide what you need in your own time at home.

The most important feature of the cord used for ornamental knots is that it should be firm: not too limp, nor too stiff, but somewhere in between. To test this, make a loop with the cord. It should hold the loop firmly without flopping, but it should not be so stiff that you cannot change the shape when it becomes necessary.

In the projects in this book I have used 2mm satin cord, some 1mm satin cord, 1mm and 1.5mm leather cord and braided cord in various thicknesses.

Satin cord is excellent for decorative knots as it is firm, easy to handle, slightly shiny and can stand the handling and pulling that knot tying requires. There are two types available, one made from nylon and the other from rayon. I prefer the nylon as it is less slippery and the end can be melted for a neat finish.

Leather cord is not so forgiving because it does not share these qualities. It is fine for Celtic style knots which do not need very much pulling about, but some Chinese knots are more demanding, and leather cord is not really suitable.

Braided cord is a pleasure to use as it holds the knot well and is not slippery.

All the cords have some advantages and disadvantages and you must decide which qualities are needed for the particular project that you have in mind.

A selection of cords.

Beads and pendants

The choice of beads available now is quite mind-boggling! For knotting, it is not possible to use beads which have very small holes, so this does narrow the choice a little. Beads are available in so many different materials: wood, semi-precious stones, ceramics, polymer clay, silver, pewter, plastic, fabric, glass and even felt and paper.

One of the best types of bead for knotting is handmade fused glass and lampwork beads. These days there are many glass artists making wonderful colourful glass beads that team perfectly with knotting cords as they have nice large even holes, and the smooth vibrant glass looks so good with satin and braided cords in matching or complementary colours. There are bead fairs where you can find all sorts of beads, charity shops for unusual old beads, many bead shops have sprung up in small towns, and there are numerous mail order companies tempting us with a vast array of all types of beads. They can be very addictive and you will find yourself looking out for beads wherever you go!

Check that the beads you use have holes large enough to be suitable for the cords you use, and note that the projects in this book sometimes require you to be able to thread two cords through a bead.

Findings

Knotted jewellery does not need as many findings as regular strung-beaded necklaces do, as the adjustable sliding button knot is such a versatile finish. However when findings are needed you must make sure that the holes in the closures are large enough to thread the cords through, and also that the weight and appearance of the closure is suitable for the beads you have used: large beads need a more substantial closure and smaller beads need a smaller, more delicate clasp or toggle closure. Findings are available from the same sources as beads and cords that I have described above.

Make sure that the findings you use are suitable. More 'chunky' clasps look better with cords and knots. The findings need to have suitably large holes as well.

Other items

Scissors These should be very sharp to give you a neat end to the cords for threading through beads. Cords cut on the diagonal are easier to thread.

PVA glue This easily available white craft glue dries clear and is used to stiffen the ends of the cords. As it dries it hardens the end of the cord, which can then be used like a needle to thread the cord through the beads. It can also be diluted (ten parts water to one part glue) to brush on to the back of a knot to stiffen it slightly and keep the loops in place. It darkens the cord a little so I try to avoid using it on the front of the knot.

Paint brush This is used to brush the PVA glue on to the ends of the cords, and to brush diluted glue on to finished knots to stiffen them a little.

Lighter A cigarette lighter is very useful for sealing the ends of synthetic cords neatly and unobtrusively in knotted jewellery. The cord end should be put into the flame for a very short time (a fraction of a second). This is just long enough to seal it to give a very neat finish to the knot, but not so long that the end of the cord becomes an ugly brown knob.

Thread zapper Very good for finishing jewellery, this cuts and heat-seals synthetic cords with one 'zap'. I do not use it for thicker cords as it uses up the batteries too quickly, but it is great for thinner, more delicate cords. It is also very accurate.

Pins Used to hold the partially finished knot in place as you work out what the next move should be. They are very helpful for holding the shape of the curves as you work. Old-fashioned T pins are too coarse, and will spoil the cords, so use glass-headed sewing pins.

Tweezers I do not generally use tweezers, except to pull cords through small spaces, but they can occasionally be really useful for difficult-to-reach corners.

Instant glue gel This comes in a dispenser which allows you to put a tiny drop of superglue gel exactly where you want it, and it does not spread and spoil your work. It holds the ends of the completed knot in place and prevents the knot from coming apart during handling later on. It is less visible than stitches and much faster!

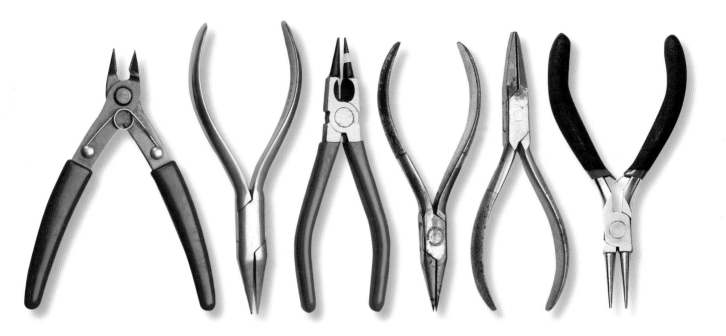

Epoxy glue You will only need this strong glue occasionally, but nevertheless it is very useful for attaching pins to completed knots to make brooches.

Bead reamer This tool is invaluable for smoothing and slightly enlarging difficult holes in beads. In some cheaper glass beads the unsightly white powdery releasing agent has not been cleaned out of the bead hole. The reamer will remove this. However, when used for this purpose the reamer must be regularly cleaned with an old toothbrush to remain effective.

Cork mat I like to use my cork mat on an adjustable laptray as I can angle the mat towards me in order to work on the knot more comfortably. The cork mat allows you to position the pins in the loops and curves of a knot and alter the placement as the knot develops. The cork is sturdy and lasts for years.

Needle A large-holed needlepoint needle with a blunt rounded end is occasionally useful when you need to thread the cord back through a button knot to finish a necklace or bracelet.

Pliers and wire cutters These are not often needed for knotted jewellery, but when you need to use a headpin or an eyepin to thread through a small-holed bead (to make an earring for example), wire cutters are needed to cut the wire and pliers to make a loop on the end of the pin. I have also used pliers to grip and pull a difficult cord through a small space.

From left: wire cutters, two pairs of needle-nosed pliers, wide flat-nosed pliers, large round-ended pliers, small round-ended pliers.

Clear nail polish Clear nail polish is very useful for stiffening cord ends quickly, as it dries hard in a few minutes. It is great when you are using beads with nice large smooth regular holes. However, if you know that you are going to have a difficult time getting your cord through the bead holes (using semi-precious stones for example, or two or more cords through one bead), it is better to use the PVA glue as it gives a much harder and stiffer end to your cord.

Tape measure To measure the length of the cord before starting your project.

A cork mat attached to a laptray.

9

Preparing cords

The best way to thread a cord through a bead is to make the end of the cord stiff so that it acts like a needle. Two stiffening methods are described on the opposite page.

Calculating lengths of cord

The following tables will help you work out how much cord to use. It is surprising how much cord is needed for decorative knots, almost always more than you had imagined! I find that as a very general rule three metres (118in) of cord is about right for most necklaces with button knots. If you find a beautiful cord you must have (before you have worked out what to use it for), then buy at least three metres; any less would probably be too short. It is better to have too much than too little cord.

Extra cord is always needed at the end of a necklace to be able to tie the last button knot, so an allowance must be made for that too. When making a necklace with more complicated knots then four metres (157½in) is a good length with which to start.

Necklace lengths

The following table lists the average length of cord you will need for different types of necklace.

Choker	40cm	(16in)
Necklace with fastener	45cm	(18in)
Necklace without fastener	70cm	(28in)

Cord lengths for knots

The following table shows the approximate length of **2mm** cord required to tie single knots.

Button knot	8.5cm	(3½in)
Sliding button knot	9.5cm	(3¾in)
Double button knot	25cm	(10in)

The following table shows the approximate length of **1mm** cord required to tie single knots.

Button knot	5.5cm	(2⅛in)
Sliding button knot	5.7cm	(2¼in)
Double button knot	15cm	(6in)

The following table shows how to determine the total length of **2mm** cord required to make an 80cm (32in) necklace with one double button knot, ten single button knots and two sliding button knots.

Length of necklace	80cm	(32in)
Double button knot	25cm	(10in)
Ten button knots	85cm	(34in)
Two sliding knots	19cm	(7½in)
Allowance for tying the sliding knots	60cm	(24in)
Total length	269cm	(107½in)

Note that it is better to have too much cord than too little, so I would add a small allowance for possible additions and cut a 3m (118in) length of cord.

Preparing cord ends

Cord ends will need to be prepared before they are used. Clear nail polish is easy to use and dries in about fifteen minutes and is good for smooth holes. PVA glue takes longer to dry, overnight is best, but it dries much harder than nail polish, so it is better for more difficult holes.

You can even make the end of the cord thinner by cutting a small sliver off the side of the stiffened end so that it goes through the bead hole more easily. Once it has appeared on the opposite side of the bead you can grip the end and pull the rest through (your pliers will be useful here). A 2mm satin cord will actually go through a hole which looks smaller than 2mm, if you have prepared the end carefully.

Cutting and stiffening 2mm cords with scissors and glue before starting

1. Use a pair of sharp scissors to cut across the cord at an angle near the end to make a point.

2. Dip a paintbrush into PVA glue and brush the end of the cord.

3. Turn the cord over and brush PVA on the other side. Leave to dry overnight. This makes a stiff 'needle' for threading.

Cutting and stiffening 2mm cords with scissors and nail polish

1. Use a pair of sharp scissors to cut across the cord at an angle near the end to make a point.

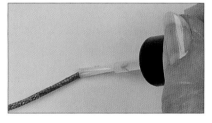

2. Use the applicator to apply nail polish to the end of the cord. Allow to dry for fifteen minutes.

Tip
Nail polish makes for a less stiff 'needle' than PVA glue, but it is very quick to dry and fine for beads with large smooth holes.

Cutting and sealing 1mm cords with a zapper to finish

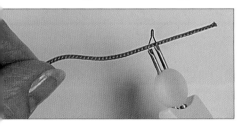

1. Feed an inch or two of cord through the cutting wire of the zapper.

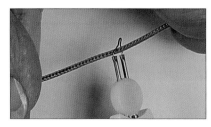

2. Grip the loose end between the first two fingers of your left hand.

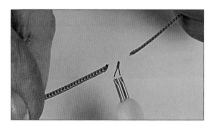

3. Hold the on/off button down and gently pull the zapper through to cut and seal the cord.

Dyeing cords

Although cords are available in many colours, it is sometimes impossible to find the exact shade that will complement your beads. Multi-purpose dyes are easily available and are fadeproof under ordinary circumstances and come in many colours. You can use these to dye white cords to a rich colour, or deepen a very pale cord to a darker shade.

It is very easy to dye cords in a microwave oven, as the cords do not take up a lot of space or need large containers.

Nylon and rayon (also known as acetate or viscose) dye easily, as do wool, cotton, linen and silk. Polyester and polypropylene do not take ordinary dyes, but a cotton polyester mix will dye to a pale shade. Cotton piping cord takes dye very well, but not waxed cotton or linen.

Although this is not strictly dyeing, I have very successfully given a too-bright white nylon cord an antique feel by dipping it into a mug of strong hot tea (no milk!) for five minutes.

Method

You will need a large heatproof glass jug, a spoon, an old newspaper to protect the kitchen counter and rubber gloves. Wear old clothes or an apron. Wrap the cord around your hand to make a loose hank and secure it with a small piece of cord loosely tied around it.

1. Put 600ml (20 fl oz or 2½ cups) of very hot water into the jug.

2. Add ¼ tsp of dye and ½ tsp salt. Stir to make sure the dye powder dissolves completely.

3. Immerse the cord into the dye solution. Stir gently to make sure the cord is thoroughly saturated with dye solution.

4. Place in the microwave oven. Since ovens vary so much, it is not possible to give the power needed for your particular oven to keep the solution simmering. It will be a low or medium setting as you definitely do not want the solution to boil over.

5. After five minutes, check the colour and stir the dye. Most manufacturers recommend dyeing for twenty minutes, but it seems to dye much more quickly in the microwave.

6. When you have achieved the colour you want (do not forget it looks much darker when wet) remove the cord from the solution, rinse it and leave it still wound up flat on the newspaper to dry.

A selection of hand-dyed cords.

Tying knots

Here we are using a very well-known and elegant knot, the Josephine knot, as an example of how to tie and tighten. This knot, also known as the double coin knot, is used in the double coin knot necklace on pages 39–41) and the epaulette knot bracelet on pages 152–157.

Weaving the knot

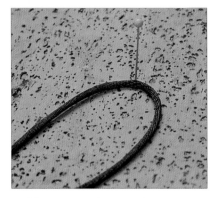

1. Pin your cord to a cork mat, making sure that the pin goes through the cord. (Note that leather cord should not be pinned. See page 153 for how to secure it.)

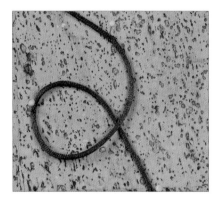

2. As you begin to make the knot, follow the diagrams carefully. Pin through the cord where convenient in order to hold the loops in place.

3. Continue the knot, making sure that you take the cord under and over according to the diagrams. Pin where convenient until the knot is loosely completed.

Tightening the knot

1. For a simple knot such as this example, remove all of the pins except for the pin marking the centre of the knot. This acts as an anchor.

2. With the pins removed, gently tug parts of the knot to tighten it, starting from the centre. Ease the cord through in small movements.

3. Continue the gradual process of tightening. Try to keep the tension even throughout the knot, rather than getting one isolated part tight. When you are satisfied with the knot, remove the anchoring pin.

Button knots

This knot is best known as a Chinese button knot. However, its round shape is typical of Celtic style, and its endless cyclical design symbolises the eternal cycle of life in both Chinese Buddhist and Celtic traditions.

The button knot is an incredibly useful knot for making jewellery as it is such an elegant and useful knot for finishing and hiding the ends of the cords. It is my favourite knot, and as such, I make no apology for the fact that it features in a number of the projects in this book.

Single button knot necklace

The necklace project on the following pages is a good way to practise making button knots. It is finished with Keren's sliding knot (see page 18), making the necklace adjustable and very versatile.

You will need

2m (78¾in) 1mm satin cord
Ten large decorative beads
One toggle clasp

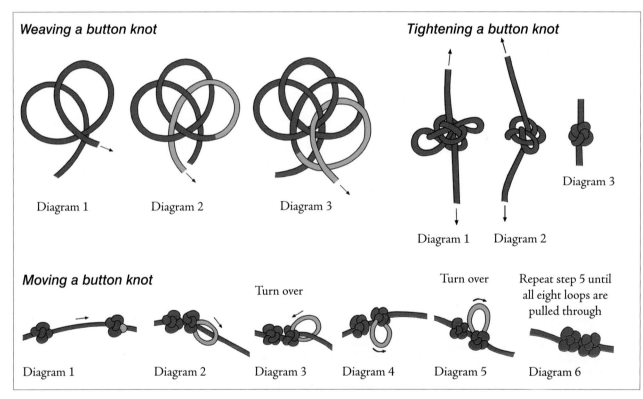

Weaving a button knot

Diagram 1   Diagram 2   Diagram 3

Tightening a button knot

Diagram 3

Diagram 1   Diagram 2

Moving a button knot

Diagram 1   Diagram 2   Turn over   Diagram 3   Diagram 4   Turn over   Diagram 5   Repeat step 5 until all eight loops are pulled through   Diagram 6

Tip

Sliding knots can be slid back and forth to adjust the length of a necklace. To do so, tie a button knot around the cord of the opposing side of a necklace, as shown.

Note that exactly the same method of tying a button knot around another cord is used to finish a necklace, although it will not necessarily slide.

Sliding button knots used with a fastener. This knot is tied around the cord on the same side of the necklace. This method also makes your necklaces adjustable.

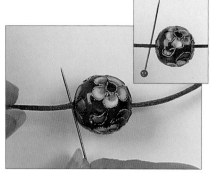

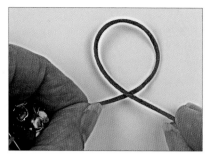

1. Stiffen the ends of the cords (see page 11), then thread a bead on to one end of the cord, as though threading a needle.

2. Fold the cord in half to find the halfway point, then run the bead down the cord until it sits in the centre. Push a pin through the cord to the left of the bead to hold it in place.

3. Make a loop to the right of the bead, taking the cord over itself.

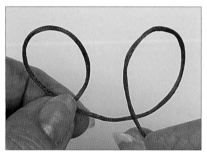

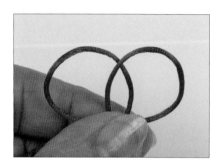

4. Holding the first loop between your thumb and index finger, make a second loop to the right.

5. Take the second loop between your thumb and index finger, on top of the first loop. See diagram 1 for weaving a button knot.

6. Take the right-hand end of the cord down through the loop on the right-hand side.

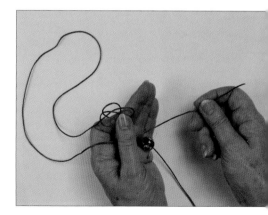

7. Take the end back up through the area where the two loops overlap one another.

8. Take the end down through the loop on the left and ease the cord through on the right-hand side just enough to make a third loop as shown. See diagram 2 for weaving a button knot.

9. Keeping hold of the knot in your left hand, take the end through the gap between your left thumb and forefinger as shown.

15

10. Pull the cord through, then take the end down through the third (new) loop.

11. Bring the end up through the lower part of the central loop, just above your left thumb.

12. Pull the cord through to begin to secure the knot. See diagram 3 for weaving a button knot.

13. Release the loops from between your finger and thumb and take both ends between your fingers; making sure the left cord is behind the knot and the right cord is in front as shown.

14. Gently pull the cords to tighten the knot. Guide the knot to lean towards the right side. This ensures the knot will tighten correctly.

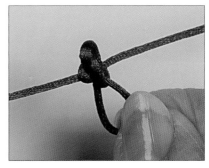

15. Identify a large loop, look for the point it re-enters the knot and pull the next loop through until the large loop lies flat against the knot.

16. Continue pulling the loops through until the button knot has taken shape.

17. Once tightened, the knot will finish about 10cm (4in) from the bead, so it needs to be moved next to the bead. Follow the cord from the bead to where it enters and leaves the knot, and pull it out while slipping the knot down towards the bead. See the diagrams for moving a button knot on page 14.

Tip
Always hold the knot in your left hand and pull the loop towards you when tightening.

18. Once the knot is adjacent to the bead, tighten it as described in steps 14–16.

19. Turn the necklace round and remove the pin, then make a second button knot on the other side of the bead.

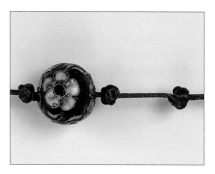

20. Make another button knot to the right of the previous one, and move it down until it is a thumb's width away from the previous knot.

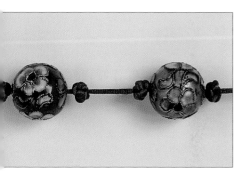

21. Thread on a blue bead and hold it in place with a second button knot.

22. Repeat this process to secure four more beads on the right and four more beads on the left as shown.

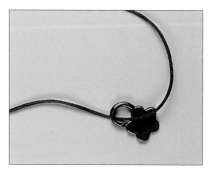

23. Thread the loop of the closure on to the left-hand end of the cord, leaving it 20cm (8in) from the end.

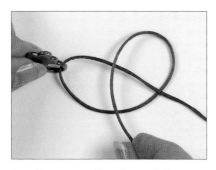

24. Now you will make a sliding button knot around the main cord. Place the clasp on the left side, then take the loose end of the cord underneath itself and round to make two overlapping loops.

25. Hold the loops in your thumb and forefinger, then take the free end around and underneath the holding cord as shown, ready to go into the loop on the right.

26. Take the end down through the right loop, up through the overlapping part and down through the left-hand loop. This makes a new, third, loop on the right.

17

27. Take the end through the gap between your left thumb and forefinger behind the holding cord again, then down through the new loop and up through the middle opening above your thumb.

28. Tighten the knot a little then move it along the cord (see page 14) so that the loop closure is in the right place before fully tightening the knot.

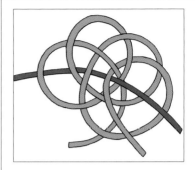

Note

This completes a sliding button knot. This knot is identical to a button knot except that it is tied around another cord. This means that the knot can be slid up and down along the cord, making it very versatile and useful.

This knot was originally a mistake by a student of mine named Keren, but it turned out to be incredibly useful and I use it all the time now.

Tip

Single button knots can be trimmed and made into a bead, then threaded on to a necklace or bracelet in exactly the same way as a regular bead.

Tip

When making a sliding button knot, the cord should always be behind the holding cord when going upwards, and in front of the holding cord when going down.

29. Tighten the sliding button knot in the same way as the button knot. Make sure that the knot is very tight.

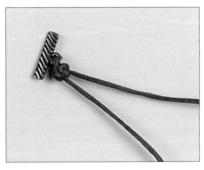

30. Secure the toggle to the other end of the cord in the same way.

31. Trim and seal the ends coming from the sliding button knots, following the instructions on page 11.

18

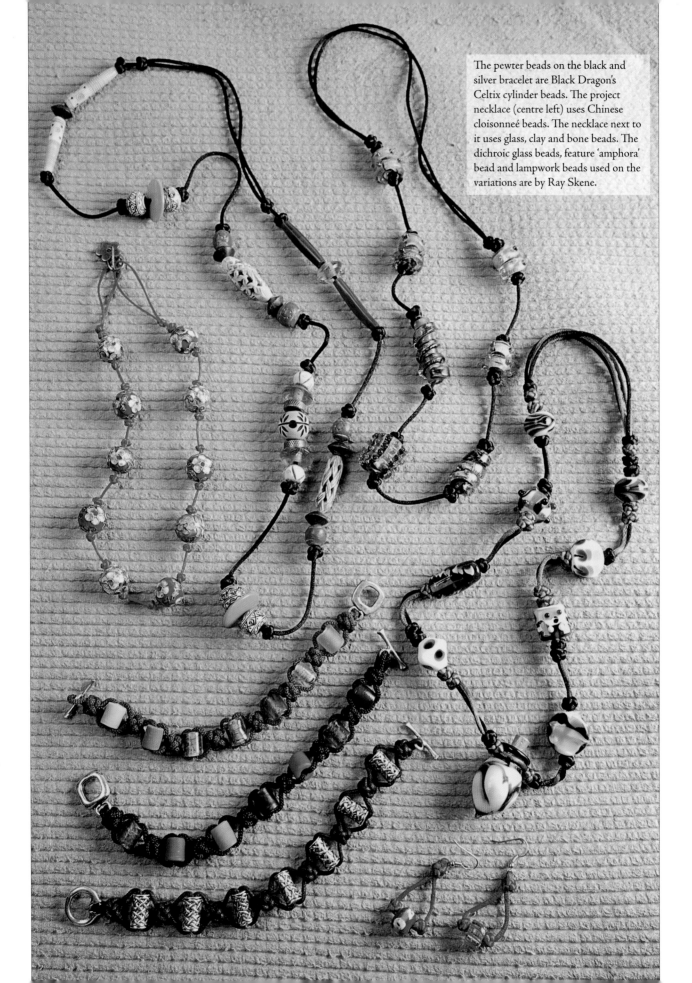

The pewter beads on the black and silver bracelet are Black Dragon's Celtix cylinder beads. The project necklace (centre left) uses Chinese cloisonneé beads. The necklace next to it uses glass, clay and bone beads. The dichroic glass beads, feature 'amphora' bead and lampwork beads used on the variations are by Ray Skene.

Tying button knots with two cord ends

Sometimes you may need to tie a knot with two cord ends: either with both ends of a single cord (to make a loop on one side of the knot), or with the ends of two different cords threaded through beads. Practise tying the knot using both ends of a 1m (39in) length of cord.

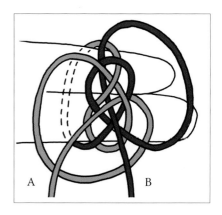

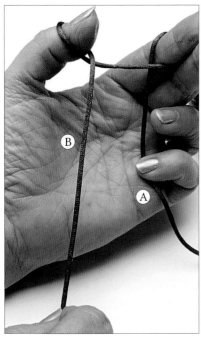

1. Place the middle of the cord behind your index finger and anchor cord end (A) with your little finger. Take cord end (B) round your thumb and back over itself. You now have two loops.

2. Lift the loop off your thumb.

3. Turn the loop over (as with a page of a book) and place it on top of the loop on your index finger.

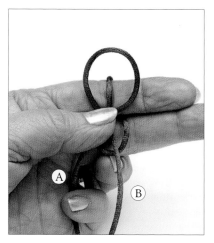

4. Anchor the cords as shown, using your thumb.

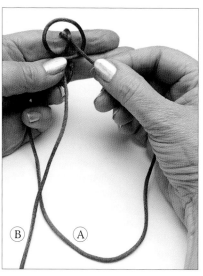

5. Check that cord A is under cord B, then thread the end of cord A through the loop on your index finger as shown.

6. Pull the end of the cord A upwards through the loops to make an open basket shape.

7. Bring cord end A down under cord B, then take it up through the middle of the basket shape.

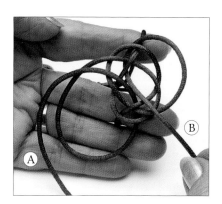

8. Pull cord A to leave a loop at the left-hand side of the basket shape. Take cord B round to the top of the basket, over the loop on the index finger and up through the centre of the basket shape to leave another loop on the right-hand side.

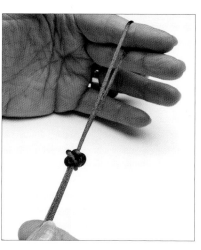

9. Check that all the overs and unders are correct (see diagram opposite), then pull both cords to close the knot.

21

Chinese Knots

My husband and I went to live in Hong Kong in 1990, and it proved to be a fascinating experience. This section is about knotting, so I can only mention in passing the wonderful restaurants, the harbour, the skyline, the Star Ferry . . . the list could go on and on! Yu Hwa, a Chinese department store, was overwhelming, with wonderful silks, porcelain, paintings, rosewood furniture, beautiful jewellery with semi-precious stones, Chinese herbal medicines and exotic food – a trip up the escalator, from the basement to the top floor, was a feast for the eyes! But my favourite place was the Jade Market in Kowloon, an unprepossessing market full of little stalls under canvas awnings, unbearably hot in Hong Kong's humid summers, but so interesting that one almost forgot the discomfort in the excitement of the place! They sold jade items (beads, pendants, necklaces and bracelets), silver and gold jewellery and an abundance of other beautiful items. One had to bargain for a good deal, and a rule of thumb (for people who are not expert on precious stones) was not to believe anyone and not to spend a large sum of money on any item.

It was at this market that I was introduced to Chinese knots. I found a stall holder sitting next to her table effortlessly knotting cord with beads. She only had enough English to tell me the price and to assure me that the beads were real jade, real amber, etc., and she certainly did not expect to show me how she did the knots!

Where was I to learn? None of my friends or acquaintances knew how to do them, and I could not find any courses or lessons, certainly not in English. I finally came across a beautiful book written in English, but the instructions were too complicated for me (then an utter novice) to learn the basics. Although I managed to tie some of the knots, I could not work out how to get them in the correct place, or how to finish a necklace. So I resigned myself to remaining mystified!

Several years later we moved to another neighbourhood and, while out shopping, I found a little shop, tucked away behind a supermarket, that sold necklaces with beads and pendants. I started chatting with the owner, whose English was very good, and one day I asked her if she could teach me how to tie Chinese knots. 'Yes', she said, 'there are details of the lessons on that notice in the window.' Of course, you have guessed it, the notice was all in Chinese! Anyway, I took a series of lessons and learned all about the famous button knot – the various ways of tying it, how to move its position on the cord and how to combine it with other knots. From then on I was hooked and I started searching for beads with large holes, and knotting necklaces with pendants and Chinese coins.

The adventure had begun!

Amber pendant necklace with a prosperity knot tied with black and rust-brown cord (see page 44).

Chinese knots are usually tied with a beautiful silky cord known by the unglamorous name of rattail! This cord is very decorative in itself and a single Chinese knot tied with it can be large, showy and complete in itself. Add a few more knots and some beads and you have an original necklace that is much stronger than a silver or gold chain. As well as being unique and valuable, your knotted necklaces can be as elegant or extravagant, and as understated or overstated as you want them to be!

To my mind, the simplicity of one beautiful knot is enough; it can satisfy our souls in a way that something more complex cannot. I think that one simple knot, or a series of knots and beads is incredibly elegant, and being able to create it yourself is a wonderful antidote to our fast-paced high-tech lives!

The most frequently used knot is the button knot. Most people have seen this knot at some time or another as little buttons on traditional Chinese dresses and jackets. On first seeing it, one wants to examine it more carefully and to meditate over its seemingly endless weaving in and out of itself in a perfect ball. In Chinese tradition this endless pattern is considered a symbol of good luck – the wearer's longevity and nobility will continue forever with great vitality! It is a graphic representation of the cyclical nature of all existence in Chinese Buddhism.

In this section, I try to demystify this interesting little knot and to show you how it can be used in various ways to make unique, elegant, handmade necklaces, bracelets and earrings.

This decorative knot can also be very functional. Pairs of button knots can be made to slide along the cord allowing a necklace to be lengthened or shortened at will. This method of closure eliminates the need for special findings to finish a necklace, and the same necklace can be a choker or a long necklace.

The button knot (see pages 14–18), with all its variations, is my favourite knot. However, I hope you will enjoy all of these Chinese-themed projects, whatever knot they use. When you have practised tying the knots and become more confident and adventurous, I am sure you will soon start to work up your own designs.

Below, from left to right:

An earring featuring a pan chang knot, beads (one of which is covered with a matching material) and a tassel.

Turquoise pendant necklace, featuring double button knots and Thai silver beads.

An earring embellished with a plafond knot and a button knot.

History

Chinese knotting (and other Chinese folk crafts) came perilously close to being entirely lost during the last century. Traditionally, Chinese women handed down craft lore from generation to generation, but, as it was never recorded as written instructions, it all but disappeared. Relics could be found in Chinese museums, but they were usually labelled as 'a tradition that we used to have'.

It is difficult to say when ornamental knotting started in China. Fabrics and cords are not as durable as the materials used in other arts and crafts, so early examples of Chinese knots have long turned to dust. Knotted rope belts, however, are known to have existed as long ago as 1122BC (the Chou dynasty). Pictures from the Han dynasty (200BC–220AD) show knots and bows on waist sashes; recently, decorative loops and knots have been found in tombs from that era. From 618 to 906AD knotting was beginning to be used to adorn other works of art, but the height of its popularity came during the Ching dynasty (1644 to 1911AD), when knots adorned clothes, jewellery, furniture and other belongings of all classes, from rich to poor.

At the beginning of the nineteenth century, the pastime of knotting was widespread and, especially on festivals and at weddings, beautiful knotwork created by the participants could be seen everywhere. The designs of the knots were fashioned after the symbols of happiness, longevity, Buddhist treasures and prosperity etc. Sadly these skills disappeared within two generations.

In the mid 1970s, however, with the increasing prosperity of Taiwan, several young Chinese artists, notably Lydia Chen and Nelson T. J. Chang, realised the importance of preserving this dying art form. At the same time, Wang Chen-Kai, a master knotter from China, began working at the National Palace Museum in Taipei. The Echo Publishing Company of Taipei succeeded in finding a few of the remaining 'keepers' of the knotting tradition. With trembling hands, these elderly people showed the youngsters how to tie the knots. After much dedicated research and lots of practice these young people revived the craft, taught it to others, recorded instructions and published books. The interest they generated was beyond their wildest expectations. In Taipei, Nelson Chang opened a large store selling knotted products. The store also contains a museum with a stunning exhibition of complex knotted works. Nowadays, there are classes in schools and colleges, and also television programmes about knotting. Thus, in the nick of time, the art of knotting, along with other Chinese folk crafts, was saved.

Traditional Chinese hanging featuring, from top to bottom: double connection knot; round brocade knot; double button knots; large pan chang knot, known as a reunion knot; a lion dog to frighten away evil spirits; and many firecracker knots, also to frighten evil spirits.

Tying Chinese knots

Before starting on a project, practise tying the knots using a 1m (39in) length of cord. Some knots can be tied in the hand, but others are best planned out on a cork mat and temporarily held in place with pins while you work out where the end should go next – you will find it easier to follow the step-by-step sequence without losing your place.

To help you even more, fix an enlarged copy of the knotting layout on the cork mat; you should have enough space to follow the instructions and maintain the correct proportions of the knot.

The shape of the knot is determined by the way the knotting is tightened. This is the most crucial part of Chinese knotting, and it can make or break your knot. It is most important to tighten a knot slowly and carefully, and to work each section of the cord as evenly and accurately as possible. Where necessary, I have included arrows on the diagrams to show you the directions in which to pull the cord.

Study the layout of each knot before you start, and make a mental note of the path of each part of the cord before you pull it tight. Always start tightening from the point where you began to tie the knot, methodically working out the slack, loop by loop, until you reach the end of the knot, repositioning the pins as necessary to retain the shape.

If a kink develops, work it out by gently twisting the cord as you tighten.

The final form of the knot is determined by how tight you make the loops; this is your decision, but I suggest that loose knots with long loops are not practical for necklaces and bracelets. Knots with short even loops (or no visible loops at all) are more suitable, and they are better at keeping their shape.

Pinning the cord to a cork mat helps to maintain the shape of the knotting.

Removing some of the pins will become necessary to weave the cord over and under itself.

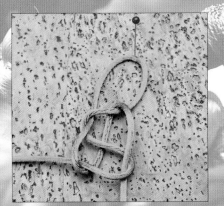

Tighten the knot gently and slowly.

Working from the starting point, pull the cords through the knot to maintain the shape of the top loop.

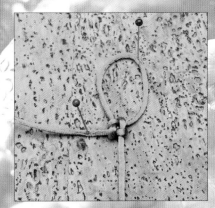

The finished knot. Its final shape depends on the tightness of the cords.

Button knots

Double button knot pendant necklace

The button knot is my favourite knot, and I hardly ever make a necklace without using at least one of them. This necklace incorporates two double button knots, made by simply doubling the cords as you work, as part of the centre pendant design and single button knots on each side. The finished necklace, which is fastened with sliding button knots, will be 88cm (34in) long.

You will need

260cm (102in) 2mm satin cord
Large circular pendant
Medium round decorative Thai silver bead
Two Thai decorated long bicone-shaped silver beads

1. Centre the large pendant on the cord, then, referring to pages 14–16, use the doubled cord to make a button knot.

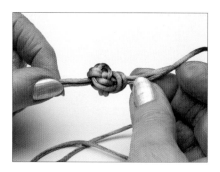

2. Carefully pull the knot tight, ensuring that the two cords sit side by side right through the knot.

3. Referring to page 16, move the knot tight against the bead.

4. Thread a round bead on both lengths of cord, then repeat steps 1–3 to work another double knot against this bead.

5. Separate the cords, then make single button knots on each cord. Thread a long bead on each side, then secure in place with another button knot. Finally, equalise the remaining lengths of cord, then make sliding button knots on each end (see page 17).

Opposite

Necklaces tied with double button knots (from left to right): African green powder glass beads; antique African head pendant; the finished project necklace; amber pendant; and Tibetan carnelian beads.

Double button knot necklace

This necklace, tied with a single length of cord, has double, single and sliding button knots interspersed with unpolished amethyst beads. Prepare the cord ends (see page 11) to help thread the cord back through the knot.

You will need

3m (118in) 2mm satin cord
Seven unpolished amethyst beads

1. Anchor a bead at the middle of the cord, then, referring to pages 14–16, tie a loose knot and move it up close to the bead.

2. Start to weave the cord back through the knot, following the lead of the original cord...

3. ...pull the new cord through the loop, keeping it uncrossed by the side of the original cord...

4. ...rotate the knot, then take the cord end through the next loop.

5. Continue rotating the knot, passing the cord under five single loops, then three double loops to finish the knot.

6. Make a second double button knot on the other side of the bead.

7. Make another double button knot and move it to leave a short length of cord between it and its neighbour. Thread on a bead, then make another double button knot.

8. Work the remaining lengths of the necklace with single button knots either side of a bead. Equalise the lengths of cord, then finish with sliding button knots (see page 17).

Opposite

Necklaces and earrings made with double button knots tied with one cord end (from left to right): necklace with dark blue Venetian glass lamp beads; earrings with handmade red glass beads; necklace with maroon horn beads and Greek ceramic round beads; the finished project necklace; and a matching pair of amethyst earrings.

Three-colour button knot bracelet

The button knots on this bracelet are all single button knots tied with one end of a cord around two different coloured cords.

1. Tie a simple overhand knot with all three cords, 7.5cm (3in) from one end.

2. Referring to page 17, use the yellow cord to make a single button knot round the other cords.

You will need

1.5m (59in)
2mm satin cord*
of each colour
Bar and ring
toggle fastener

* For a two-colour bracelet use
180cm (71in) of cord for each colour.

3. Move the knot up against the overhand knot, then use the red cord to make a knot round the yellow and brown cords.

4. Move the red knot up against the yellow one, then make a brown knot round the red and yellow cords.

5. Move the brown knot up against the red one, then repeat steps 2–4 to continue the sequence of knots. When the bracelet is long enough, pass two cord ends through the ring half of the fastener.

6. Thread the end of one cord in a large-eyed tapestry needle, then pass it back through three knots.

7. Repeat step 6 with the other cord, but, this time take it back through just two knots.

8. Trim all three cords to leave just 2–3mm (⅛in), then seal the ends with a flame. Repeat steps 5–8 at the other end of the bracelet with the toggle half of the fastener.

The finished project bracelet, together with similar bracelets in other colourways.
Some of these are tied with three cords, others with just two.

Flat button knot

This variation of the button knot is tied with one end of a cord, which allows a series of knots to be tied side by side. A single flat button knot at one end of a necklace can be inserted through a large loop at the other end to form the closure (see pages 35–36). The finished knot, especially when worked with silky cords, may need a stitch or two on the back to stop it from twisting or loosening.

Flat button knot.

Tying the knot

This knot can be tied in the hand, but I suggest you practise tying it on a cork mat. If you want to tie the knot with two cords side by side, as shown opposite, a cork mat is essential. In the diagrams below, previous knots would be on cord A.

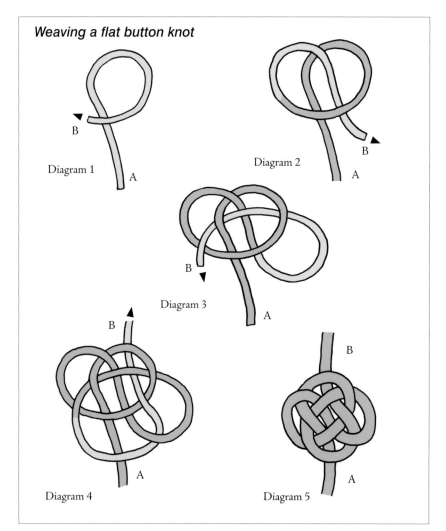

Weaving a flat button knot

Diagram 1

Diagram 2

Diagram 3

Diagram 4

Diagram 5

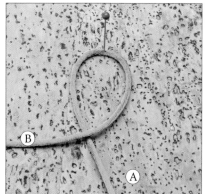

1. Anchor cord A, then form a loop with cord B (diagram 1).

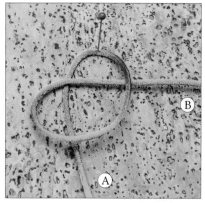

2. Take cord B round and down through the loop (diagram 2).

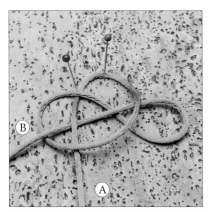

3. Form a loop, then weave cord B under, over, under and over the knotting (diagram 3).

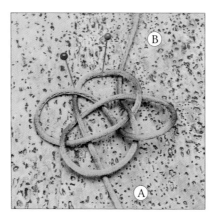

4. Take cord B round over cord A, then weave it under, over, under and under the knotting (diagram 4).

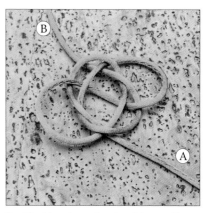

5. Start to close the knot by pulling both ends of the cord.

6. Remove the knot from the pin board, then pull the cord through the knot to equalise the loops. At this point, if you wish, you can move the knot along the cord.

7. Continue adjusting the size of the loops until you are happy with the shape of the knot.

Tying the knot with two cords

The flat button knot can also look very good when tied with two cords. You can follow the step-by-step sequence, working with both cords at once, or you can work the knot with a single cord up to step 4, then weave the second cord through the knotting. Which ever way you choose to work, ensure that the cords are not allowed to twist over each other. They must sit flat and side by side throughout the knot.

Cross knot

In Chinese a cross simply means ten. This knot gives a nice round loop and is very stable. It can also look very attractive as a sequence of knots tied with two different colours.

Tying the knot

This knot is best tied on a cork mat, with pins holding the shape of the loops. In the diagrams below, the knot is tied using two cord ends, A and B, but it can also be tied with just one cord end by starting at point D in diagram 3.

Front and back views of a cross knot.

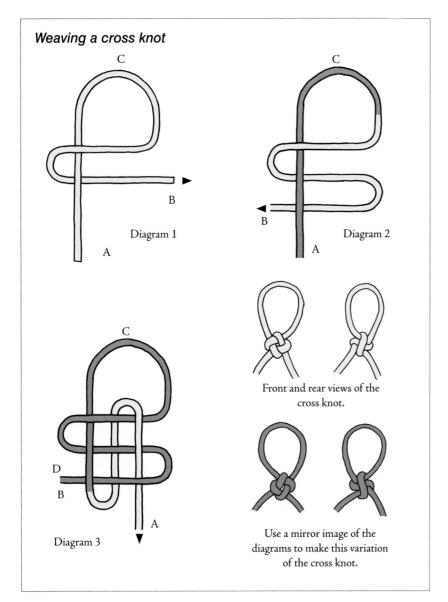

Weaving a cross knot

C

B

Diagram 1

A

C

B

Diagram 2

A

Front and rear views of the cross knot.

Use a mirror image of the diagrams to make this variation of the cross knot.

C

D

B

A

Diagram 3

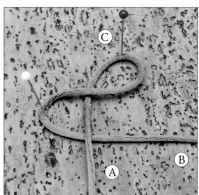

1. Anchor the middle of the cord at point C, and cord A at the bottom of the cork board. Form a U-bend with cord B taking it over then back under cord A (diagram 1).

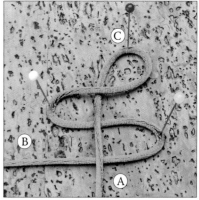

2. Form another U-bend, anchor this with a pin, then take cord B under cord A (diagram 2).

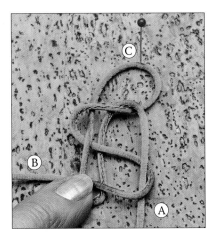

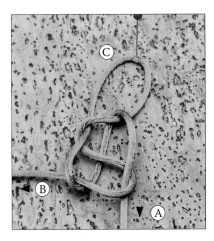

3. Anchor cord B, then take cord A up under the two U-bends in cord B, then back down, over two cords and under the third (diagram 3).

4. Start to close the knot by pulling cords A and B gently in the directions indicated.

5. Before fully tightening the knot, adjust the size of the top loop (or the position of the knot relative to previous ones) by pulling cord A and then cord B through the knot.

Cross knot necklace with flat button knot fastener

This attractive necklace consists of a series of cross knots with beads threaded between each knot and is tied with leather cord. Use pairs of pins to secure each loop of the knot to the cork mat – single pins through the leather could leave unsightly marks.

The fastener is a flat button knot, also worked on the cork mat, which engages the first loop of the necklace.

You will need

2m (79in), 1.5mm diameter leather cord

Twelve rectangular tube beads

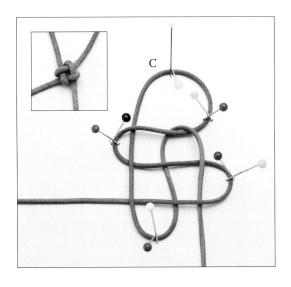

1. Referring to the diagrams opposite, build up an open cross knot on a cork mat. Carefully pull the knot tight, leaving a 3cm (1¼in) loop above the knot. You may find it helpful to reposition the pins that anchor each loop as the knot is pulled tighter.

Tightening tip
Keep the centre of the knot pattern flat as you tighten the knot, or you could lose its shape.

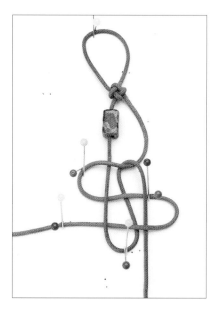

2. Thread a bead on the left-hand cord, then repeat step 1 to make another cross knot.

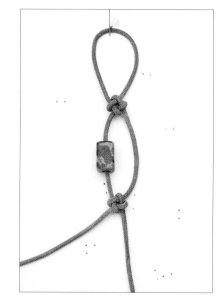

3. Pull this knot tight, leaving 3cm (1¼in) lengths of cord between it and the first knot. Repeat steps 1–3, keeping the loops between the knots evenly spaced, until the necklace is 43cm (17in) long.

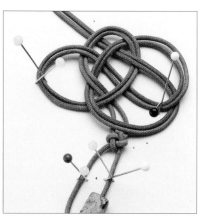

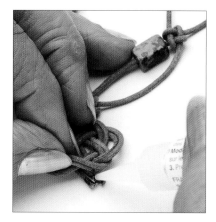

4. Referring to the diagrams on page 32, build up a double flat knot at the end of the necklace. Work on the cork mat and use pairs of pins to hold the cords flat.

5. Keeping both cords side by side, carefully pull the knot closed, tight up against the final cross knot.

6. Trim off the excess ends of the cords, then use instant glue to stick the trimmed ends to the underside of the knot.

7. Finally, using touches of instant glue, secure the beads in the middle of the loops.

Opposite

Bracelets and necklaces made with cross knots.
From left to right:
Bracelet made using four cords. The cross knots were tied first with the outside pairs of cords then with the middle two cords. The cord ends were unravelled to make the tassel.

Bracelet with blue and green beads threaded along the cord between the cross knots.

The finished project necklace.

Dark brown leather necklace, again with a flat button knot and loop fastening.

Double coin knot

This is a well known knot which, in the West, is referred to as the Josephine knot. To the Chinese, the shape represents two overlapping antique coins and denotes great prosperity and long life. It is often hung over the entrances to shops and businesses to attract lots of customers and hence a good income.

A series of these knots tied side by side with one end of a firm cord looks lovely. The introduction of a second, different coloured cord can be very attractive. A variation of the knot, tied with both ends of the cord gives a series of knots one above another. The knot can also be used to join to cords (see page 40).

Double coin knot.

Tying the knot with one end of a cord

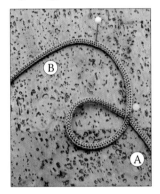 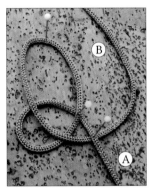 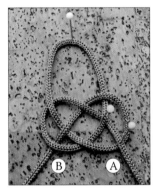 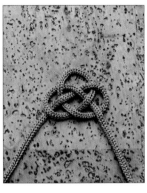

1. Anchor the right-hand cord at A and form a loop with cord end B. Use pins to hold the shape.

2. Form a second loop by taking cord B down over the first loop, then under the right-hand cord.

3. Complete the knot pattern by weaving cord B down through the two loops as shown.

4. Remove the pins and gently pull the knot into its final shape.

Tying the knot with two ends of a cord

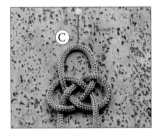 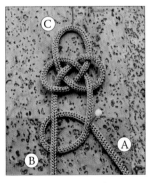 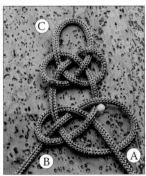 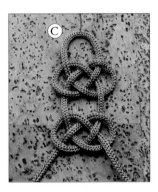

1. Anchor the centre of the cord at point C, then use both cord ends to tie a knot as shown above.

2. Form a loop with the right-hand cord A.

3. Take cord B round under cord A, then weave it down through the two loops as shown.

4. Gently pull the knot into the correct shape.

Double coin knot necklace

Double coin knots are not very stable when tied with soft cord so I used firm braided cord for this project. Pay particular attention to the spacing and tightening of the knots; they should be equally spaced and all the same size. The necklace has a hook and eye fastener.

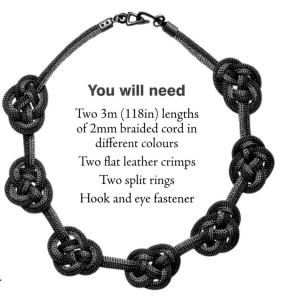

You will need

Two 3m (118in) lengths of 2mm braided cord in different colours

Two flat leather crimps

Two split rings

Hook and eye fastener

Leather crimp, split ring and the hook part of the fastener.

1. Referring to the step-by-step photographs opposite, anchor the right-hand end of the pair of cords and build up a double coin knot keeping the cords side by side.

2. Release the pin in the top loop, then tighten the knot by closing the loops as shown.

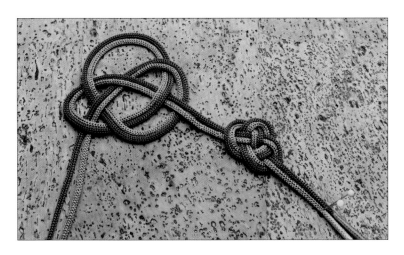

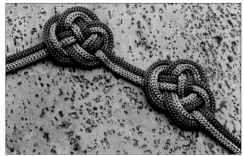

3. Working with the left-hand ends of the cords, build up a second knot. Tighten this knot to leave a short length of cords between it and the first knot.

4. Continue making knots until the necklace is long enough, then place the leather crimp on one end of the bracelet. Use a pair of pliers to clamp first one side then the other of the leather crimp.

5. Trim off the excess cords, then flame seal the exposed ends.

6. Use two pairs of pointed pliers to twist the ends of the split ring apart.

7. Secure the hook fastener to the leather crimp with the split ring. Repeat steps 4–7 to finish the other end of the necklace.

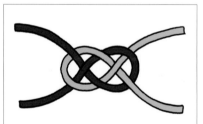

This variation of the double coin knot can be used to join two lengths of cord.

Opposite

The finished project necklace and a matching necklace and bracelet set. The double coin knots used for this set were tied with two ends of two cords.

Double connection knot

This is a very stable knot and looks especially good when it is tied with two different coloured cords.

Tying the knot

Double connection knot.

1. Tie an overhand knot with the brown cord to form a loop enclosing the black cord.

2. Tie an overhand knot with the black cord to form a loop within the brown loop.

3. Arrange the two loops as shown.

4. Close the knot by pulling both cords at each end.

Prosperity knot

This knot takes its name from the fact that it has the appearance of a large number of double coin knots woven together. It looks best with a second cord of a different colour added after the tying of the first cord is complete. Although it can be used on its own, it does look good with a pendant attached. In this case, the pendant must be threaded on the cord before the knot is tied.

Prosperity knot tied with two colours.

Tying the knot

Allow 40cm (16in) of cord for the knot itself, plus enough for the rest of the necklace. Practise tying the knot with a 1m (39in) length of cord. I find the simplest way to tie this knot is to prepare a cork mat with seven pins arranged as shown; the columns are approximately 7cm (2¾in) apart and the rows 3cm (1½in) apart.

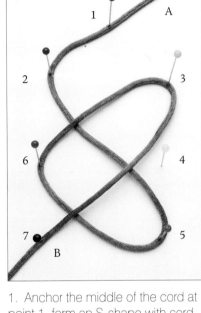

1. Anchor the middle of the cord at point 1, form an S-shape with cord end B and anchor this at points 2, 7 and 3. Take the cord back over itself and anchor it to points 5 and 4.

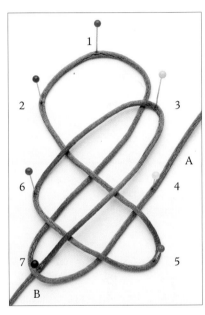

2. Pass the cord end A under the existing lay of the cord down to point 4. Take it over the cord at this point, then back up, under the existing lay of the cord, to point 6.

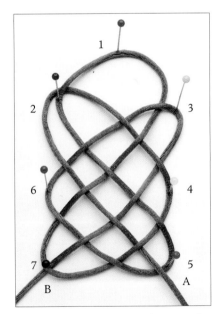

3. Now weave the end of the cord A over and under the existing lay of the cord, up and round point 2 then back down to point 7.

4. Check all the under and overs, then remove the pins and pull the knot to the required size.

Prosperity knot and double connection knot necklace

Black and rust-brown are the perfect match for the amber pendant of this lovely necklace. The shape of the pendant and the prosperity knot are balanced by the delicate shape of the double connection knots used to form the sides of the necklace. Double sliding button knots are used to close the necklace and make the length adjustable.

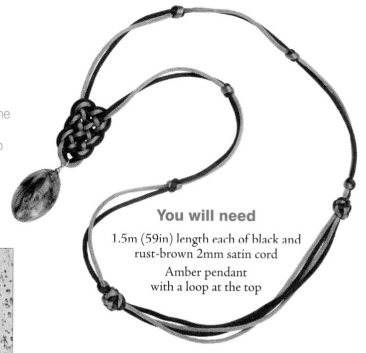

You will need

1.5m (59in) length each of black and rust-brown 2mm satin cord

Amber pendant with a loop at the top

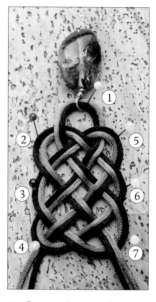

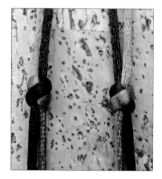

1. Centre the pendant on both cords and pin the middle of the cords to point 1. Referring to the instructions on page 43, weave an open knot. Keep the knotting flat with the cords side by side.

2. Remove the pins and gently pull the knot tight.

3. Referring to the instructions on page 42, make double connection knots with each pair of cords. Note that the left-hand knot has the black cord on top and the right-hand one the brown cord on top. Move the knots to leave 8cm (3¼in) between them and the prosperity knot.

4. Make a second set of double connection knots, 8cm (3¼in) away from the first set, then a third set another 8cm (3¼in) along the cord. Equalise the lengths of cord, then, referring to page 17, make a double sliding button knot on each end. Trim off excess cord and seal the ends with a flame.

Opposite
The finished project necklace and a bracelet with wooden beads set between prosperity knots.

Clover leaf knot

This knot is tied with one end of a cord, which makes it very versatile. The knot consists of inner U-bends and outer 'leaf' loops and is best tied on a cork mat. The number of loops can be varied from two up to five or six. For this reason, the knot is also known as a flower knot. It is very attractive and is often used as the basis of more complicated Chinese combination knots. A four-leaved clover, for example, is considered to be very lucky by the Chinese. The knot is not very stable, especially when tied with a silky cord, so the body of the knot should be secured with a few stitches on the back.

Clover leaf knot.

Tying the knot

The sequence of diagrams below show how to tie a knot with four U-bends and three leaf loops, but I have also included the final stage diagram for both two- and four-leaf knots.

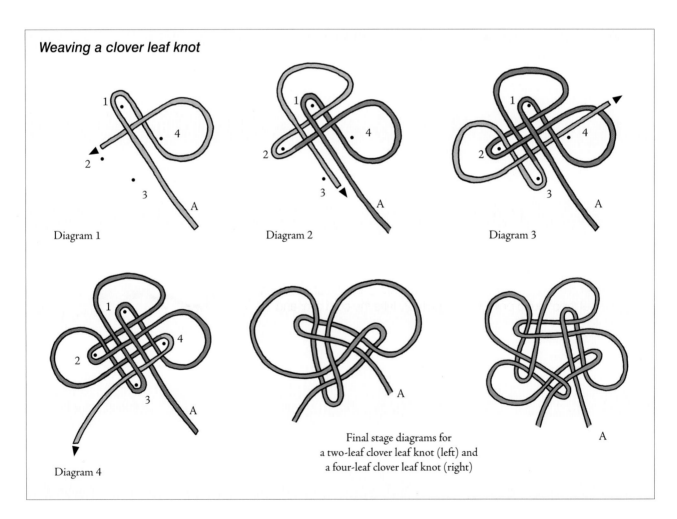

Weaving a clover leaf knot

Diagram 1

Diagram 2

Diagram 3

Diagram 4

Final stage diagrams for
a two-leaf clover leaf knot (left) and
a four-leaf clover leaf knot (right)

Clover leaf knot necklace

This necklace is approximately 96cm (38in) long and incorporates two, three-loop clover leaf knots and a series of button knots.

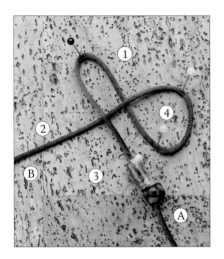

1. Referring to pages 14–16, make a single button knot, 40cm (16in) from one end of the cord, and thread a bead on the short end. Anchor cord end A, then use cord end B to make a U-bend round point 1 and a leaf loop round point 4. Take the cord over and under the U-bend and across to point 2 (diagram 1).

You will need

3m (118in) length of
2mm satin cord

Five tubular ceramic beads

One round ceramic bead

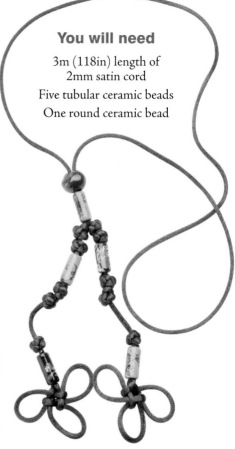

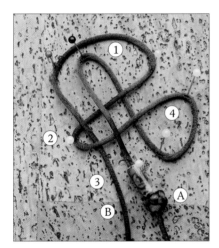

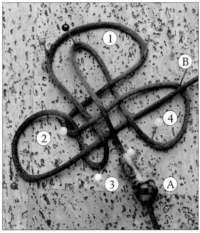

2. Make U-bend round point 2, take the cord under and over U-bend 1, and form a leaf loop round point 1. Take the cord over and under the U-bend 2 and across to point 3 (diagram 2).

3. Repeat step 2 to make a U-bend round point 3 and a leaf loop round point 2. Take the cord over and under U-bend 3 and under both cords of U-bend 1 (diagram 3).

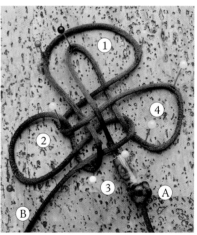

4. Make a U-bend round point 4, take the cord over both cords of U-bend 1, then under and over the cords of U-bend 3 (diagram 4).

47

5. Working from the bead end, start to close the knot by shortening the U-bends and making the leaf loops smaller.

6. Continue pulling the cord through until the centre knot is tight and the leaf loops are the same size.

7. Take the short end of the cord back through the bead, trim off the excess cord and flame seal the end between the bead and button knot.

8. Make a second button knot and move it so that it is 2cm (¾in) away from the first. Make a third button knot and move this up against the second one. Add a tubular bead, then make two more button knots. Take the cord through a third tubular bead and the round bead, leave a 40cm (16in) long neck loop, then take the cord back through the round bead and the third tubular one. Repeat the design with two button knots, a tubular bead and a further two button knots.

9. Repeat steps 1–7 to finish the necklace with a button knot, tubular bead and clover leaf knot on the other end of the cord.

Variation tip

If you insert a pair of sliding button knots in the neck loop, the necklace can be shortened to a fashionable choker length.

Opposite

The finished necklace and a matching brooch. I like asymmetrical designs, and this necklace would look just as good with one of the clover leaf knots pulled through the tubular bead to hang below the other. The brooch features a pan chang knot (see pages 54–55), with a sieve brooch-back sewn on the back, and two clover leaf knots tied below the bead.

Good luck knot

Chinese knots are considered to be tokens of love and affection. This good luck knot, like many of its fellow knots, should bring extra good fortune to the lucky wearer as well as to the giver of the knot.

Tying the knot

The diagrams below show how to tie this knot with three loops, but it can be tied with four or five loops. Theoretically even more loops are possible, but, in practice, the knotting would be almost impossible to control. A cork mat and pins are essential. The initial U-bends in the knotting should be approximately 12cm (5in) long.

Good luck knot.

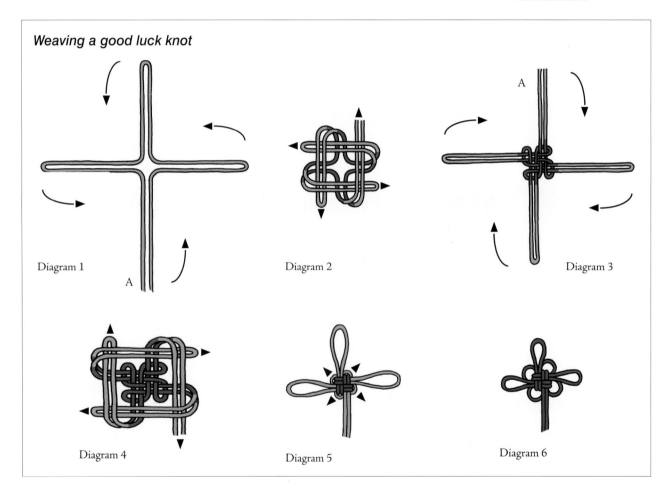

Weaving a good luck knot

Diagram 1

Diagram 2

Diagram 3

Diagram 4

Diagram 5

Diagram 6

Good luck knot pendant necklace

This necklace uses the good luck knot as a pendant. Its slightly asymmetrical shape adds to its charm and good looks. The loops are large and will keep their shape if you stiffen them with diluted PVA glue. The finished necklace (excluding the pendant) is 40cm (16in) long.

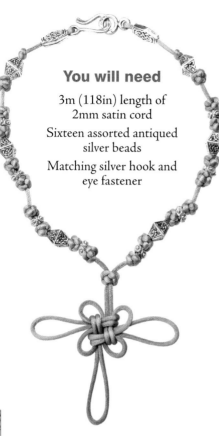

You will need

3m (118in) length of 2mm satin cord

Sixteen assorted antiqued silver beads

Matching silver hook and eye fastener

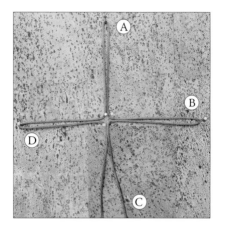

1. Fold the cord in half and pin the centre at point A. Arrange each end of the cord to form loops as shown.

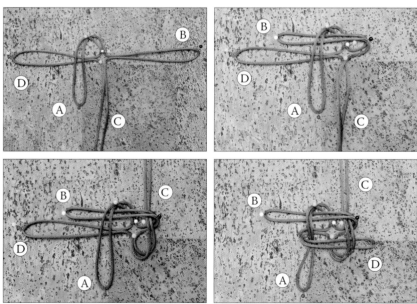

2. Fold loop A down over loop D. Fold loop B over and under the cords of loop A. Fold the cord ends C over and under the cords of loop B. Complete this step by folding loop D over and under the cords of loop C.

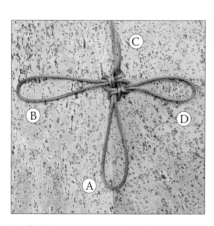

3. Pull the loops to close the knot.

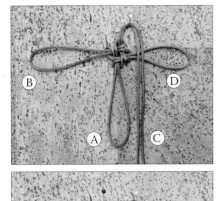

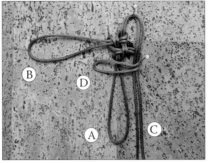

4. Now working in the opposite direction: fold cord ends C down over loop D; fold loop D over loop A; fold loop A over loop B; then complete this step by folding loop B over loop A and under loop C.

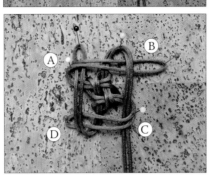

5. Pull the loops to close the knot, then pull out the small loops from the back of the knot. Adjust the large loops to size.

6. When you are happy with the shape, stiffen the back of the knot with some diluted PVA glue. Ten parts water to one part glue will stiffen the cord without affecting the colour of the cord too much.

7. Referring to page 20, use two cord ends to make a single button knot. Move this knot to leave a 1cm (½in) length of cord between it and the Good Luck knot. Working along each cord in turn, tie two groups of four single button knots separated by three beads with a short length of cord between each group. Leave a short gap, then work two single button knots separated by a bead.

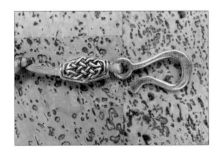

8. Equalise the ends of the cords, thread each end through a bead, through the ring of the fastener and back through the bead. Trim off excess cord, add a touch of instant glue if necessary, then flame seal the ends to complete the necklace.

Opposite

The finished project necklace and a similar necklace with matching earrings.

Pan chang knot

In Chinese, pan chang means endless. The endless pattern of this knot represents birth and death, and indicates that life can exist for ever – one of the most basic concepts of Chinese Buddhism. As one of the Eight Buddhist Treasures, it also represents the mysteries of the Universe and is also known as the Mystic Knot. As such it is considered to bring great good fortune to the wearer and beholder alike. As if this is not enough, the Chinese word for this knot shares the same sound as the word for happiness, so the knot is also taken to mean happiness without end.

Pan chang knot.

Tying the knot

The initial knotting is flat but, when the knot is tightened, the woven cords separate into the two layers, making it very stable. It looks difficult but, if you follow the overs and unders, it turns out very well. The secret is in the tightening and the outer loops must be even. Hold the square centre of the knot, and pull the outside loops equally in both directions at once, and as consistently even as possible.

   A cork mat and pins are definitely required! Practise tying the knot with a 2m (79in) length of cord. At first, try working with two different coloured cords, pinned together at point C so that, when you are tightening the knot, you can concentrate on one colour at a time.

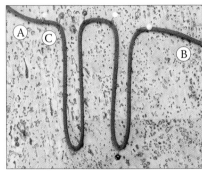

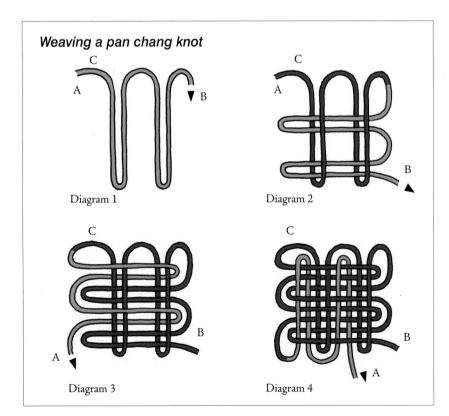

Weaving a pan chang knot

Diagram 1

Diagram 2

Diagram 3

Diagram 4

1. Secure the middle of the cord at point C and cord end A at the edge of the cork mat. Form two vertical loops with cord B (diagram 1)...

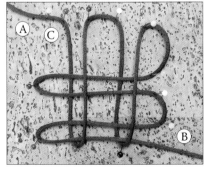

2. ... then make two horizontal loops, taking each of these under, over, under and over the vertical lengths of cord (diagram 2).

54

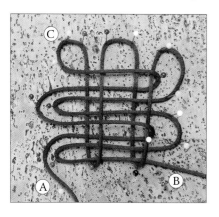

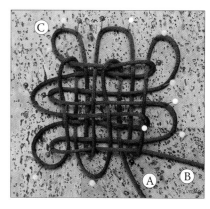

3. Now, using cord end A, lay in two further horizontal loops – work each of these loops by taking the cord over all four vertical cords, then back under them all (diagram 3).

4. Complete the knotting by weaving two further vertical loops. Check all the unders and overs are as shown in diagram 4.

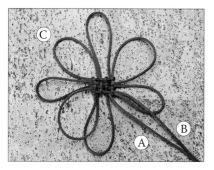

5. Close the knot by pulling on the outer seven loops. As the knot tightens, the cords that were sitting side by side, will move on top of each other.

6. Starting at point C, pull cord B through the knot to reduce the size of the loops 1–4. Now pull cord A through the knot to reduce the size of loops 5–7.

7. Repeat step 6 until all the loops are at the required size and the centre knot is neat and square. If the loops are left large, stiffen the knot with PVA glue (see page 52).

Pan chang knot necklace

This is a Western style necklace with a Chinese flavour. A pan chang knot pendant is decorated with a few beads attached to a head pin. More beads and button knots make up the sides of the necklace, the length of which is made adjustable by two sliding button knots.

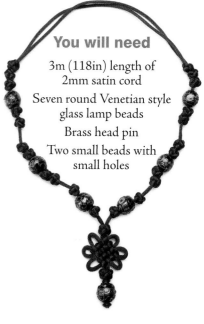

You will need

3m (118in) length of 2mm satin cord

Seven round Venetian style glass lamp beads

Brass head pin

Two small beads with small holes

1. Thread three beads on the head pin as shown.

2. Use a pair of wire cutters to trim the head pin to leave 1.5cm (½in) above the bead.

3. Use two pairs of pliers to form a ring on the end of the head pin.

4. Set the completed bead pendant in the middle of the cord.

5. Referring to pages 20–21, use both cord ends to tie a single button knot.

6. Move the button knot tight up against the bead pendant so that it covers the ring.

7. Referring to the instructions on pages 54–55, anchor the button knot at point C and tie a pan chang knot. Pull it to size, then work a second button knot with the free ends of the cords.

8. Separate the cords, then, working on each length in turn, make two button knots with a bead between them. Move this group to leave a short length of cord between it and the pendant knots.

9. Now make a group of four button knots with a bead between and move this group to leave a short length of cord between it and the first group. Repeat this step to make another group of knots.

10. Equalise the lengths of cord, then, referring to pages 17–18, make sliding button knots to complete the necklace.

Design observation

When it comes to original design, there are subtle differences between Eastern and Western ideas.

I like asymmetrical designs, and I often leave spaces between knots, but a Chinese friend told me that she did not feel comfortable with them.

She said that, traditionally, a Chinese person would not leave gaps between knots, and that symmetry is a very important aspect of Chinese design.

Opposite

The pan chang knot features in all these necklaces and earrings. Note that the loops have been pulled out in several different ways to illustrate how the shape of the knot can be altered. The button knots used along the length of the necklaces represent the worker bees, while the pan chang knot represents the queen bee of Chinese knots.

Snake knot

The snake is one of the twelve animals in the Chinese horoscope. It is regarded as a bringer of good fortune, and also the guardian of treasure. In China it is considered to be very unlucky to injure or kill a snake which comes into your house. Apparently there are not many poisonous varieties in China!

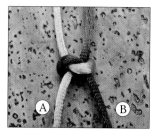

Snake knot.

Tying the knot

This is a very snakelike knot when made up and can twist and turn just like its namesake. Two cord ends are required to tie the knot. It looks good when worked with two different colours, but you can practise the knot with a 2m (79in) length of cord folded in the middle. This will make a 15cm (6in) snake. A cork mat is useful for the first few stages.

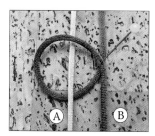

1. Make a loop with cord B, taking it under and over cord A.

2. Now make a loop with cord A, taking it over and under the first loop and back under itself.

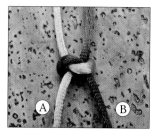

3. Gently pull both cords to close the knot.

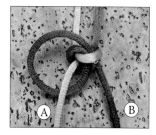

4. Take cord B under cord A and down through its loop as shown.

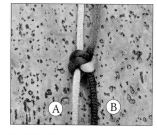

5. Gently pull cord B to close the knot. Note that the double closed loop on the left-hand side of this step only appears at the beginning of the snake.

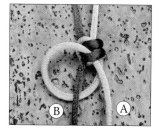

6. Turn the knotting over and take cord A under cord B and down through the lower of the two closed loops as shown.

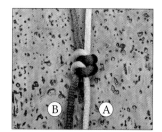

7. Gently pull cord A to close the knot.

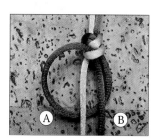

8. Turn the knotting over and repeat steps 4–7 until the snake is long enough.

When you are confident with the method of knotting and have settled into a rhythm, you will find it quicker to hold the knotting in your left hand and knot from left to right. Rotate the knotting towards you to turn it over after each knot.

Snake knot necklace

Snake knots are ideal for making a heavier than usual necklace. Here, a double coin knot, tied with two cords, supports the turquoise pendant. The central design is balanced with a button knot between two glass beads on each side. The sides are then worked with continuous snake knots. The finished necklace is approximately 44cm (17¼in) long.

You will need

Two 3m (118in) lengths of 2mm satin cord

Turquoise pendant with a top loop

Four turquoise glass beads

Hook and eye fastener

1. Thread the pendant on to both lengths of cord, anchor at the middle, then, referring to page 38, make a double coin knot.

2. Working on one side of the pendant at a time, thread both cords through a bead and make a single button knot. Move this knot up against the bead, then thread on another bead.

3. Referring to the instructions opposite make a series of snake knots until the knotting is 15cm (6in) long.

4. Attach the hook and ring fasteners to the ends in a similar manner to that described on page 30.

The finished project necklace and other variations, all of which have snake knot sides. The necklace at bottom left has a carnelian bead as the central feature, while a multicoloured handmade glass bead adorns the one at bottom right.

Necklaces and earrings using round brocade knots (see overleaf). The left-hand necklace has a handmade, fused glass pendant connected to an enlarged loop of a round brocade knot. The sides of the necklace are decorated with coloured glass beads in matching colours interspersed with button knots. The other necklace is the project on page 63. The earrings have round brocade knots with very small loops and silver beads.

61

Round brocade knot

The round pattern of this knot denotes good fortune, as, to the Chinese, a circle represents the origin of all creation, and a ring is the symbol of eternity.

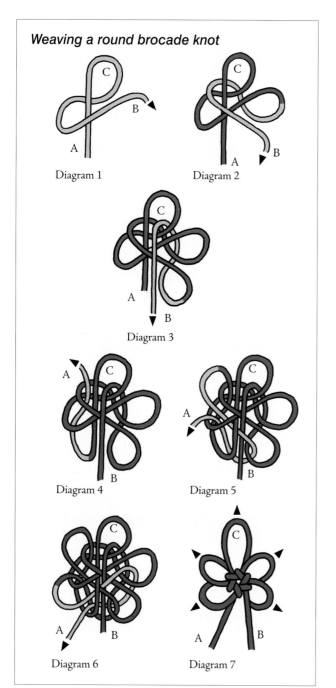

Weaving a round brocade knot

Diagram 1

Diagram 2

Diagram 3

Diagram 4

Diagram 5

Diagram 6

Diagram 7

Round brocade knot.

Tying the knot

This knot is best tied on a cork mat. It is usually tied with two working cord ends, but, if you are very patient, it is possible to tie it with one working end. Try to keep all the loops roughly equal in size so that they remain so when the knot is closed.

Start by anchoring the middle of the cord at point C and cord A at the bottom of the cork board, then take cord B under and over cord A to form the first loops (diagram 1).

Continue making loops with cord B as shown in diagrams 2 and 3, then anchor this cord.

Now, weave loops with cord A as shown in diagrams 4–6 to complete the knotting.

At this stage you can make the loops smaller by pulling the cord through from the beginning and following steps 2 to 6. Close the centre of the knot by pulling the loops as shown in diagram 7.

Round brocade knot necklace

A round brocade knot forms a pendant for this delicate necklace, the sides of which are decorated with button knots and a multitude of different coloured beads. A few small matching beads were attached to the bottom loop of the round brocade knot with a head pin. The finished necklace is approximately 41cm (16in) long.

You will need

250cm (99in) 1.5mm cord
Brass head pin
Two small brass beads
Sixty-six small beads
in assorted colours
Brass hook and loop
fastener

1. Anchor the middle of the cord at point C, then, referring to the diagrams opposite, tie a round brocade knot.

2. Referring to pages 28–29, tie two button knots with a bead between them. Move this group up close to the round brocade knot.

3. Separate the two cords, then, tie two button knots with eleven beads between them. Move this group to leave a short gap between it and the pendant knots.

4. Now work a group of two button knots and three beads. Move these to leave a gap between it and the previous group.

5. Repeat steps 3 (once) and 4 (twice), equalising the length of each side of the necklace. Take the cord end through the ring of the fastener and back through the last group of button knots and beads. Trim off the excess cord and seal the end.

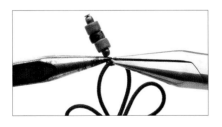

6. Finally, referring to pages 55–56, thread some beads on a head pin then use two pairs of pliers to form a ring through the loop of the round brocade knot. Stiffen the loops of the knot with diluted PVA glue (see page 52).

Virtue knot

This knot has a pattern similar to an ancient Buddhist motif that symbolises the sun, fire, the Buddha's heart, complete virtue, and power over evil. It is the sign for ten thousand, Wan Tzu, and is said to come from heaven, and stands for the accumulation of good fortune.

Virtue knot.

Tying the knot

This knot is not very stable and needs a stitch or two to keep it in shape, especially when worked with silky cord. It lends itself very well to the addition of beads on the loops.

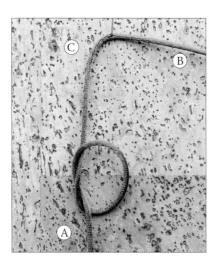

1. Anchor the middle of the cord at point C, then make an overhand knot with cord end A.

2. Make an overhand knot with cord B, taking the cord through the loop in cord A.

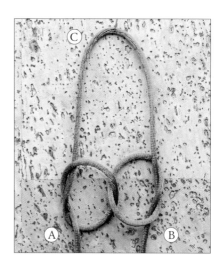

Tying variation

If the cords are pulled tight after step 2, a knot without side loops results. This is known as a true lover's knot.

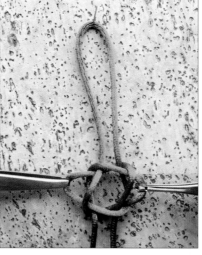

3. Pull the two loops through the overhand knots. Tweezers have been used to show the movement, but it would be better to use your fingers.

4. Continue pulling the loops to tighten the knot.

Virtue knot bracelet

A series of virtue knots, the loops of which are threaded with antique green glass beads, creates this beautiful bracelet which will glow on your wrist. The last beaded knot and the initial loop form the closure. The finished bracelet is 24cm (9½in) long.

You will need

2m (79in) 2mm satin cord
Nine large green glass beads
Sixty small blue, turquoise and green glass beads

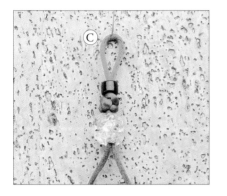

1. Anchor the middle of the cord at point C, thread on a small blue bead, then, referring to pages 20–21 use both cord ends make a single button knot. Move the knot up against the bead, leaving a 2cm (¾in) closure loop. Referring to page 36, secure the blue bead with instant glue. Thread both cords through one of the large green beads.

2. Thread three small beads on to each length of cord, then, referring to the diagram opposite, tie two entwined overhand knots; arrange the beads as shown.

3. Pull the loops and beads through the overhand knots.

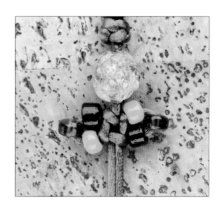

4. Pull the ends of the cords to close the knot. Pull the cords through the knot to adjust the size of the loops and position the knot tight up against the glass bead.

5. Repeat steps 2–4 until the bracelet is 24cm (9½in) long.

6. When the last virtue knot has been tightened, add a final small bead, trim off the excess cord and flame seal the end to secure the bead and finish the bracelet. The last virtue knot acts as the fastener.

The finished project bracelet together with a similar design that has single beads on the side loops of the virtue knot.

Two necklaces tied with flat knots. The bottom one, tied with two lengths of green and
two lengths of blue cord, is the project described on pages 68–69.
In the top necklace, which is tied with three colours of cord, the green cord that appears
in the centre double coin knot forms the lazy cords of the two sides.

Flat knot

This knot will be familiar to readers as the western square knot, or reef knot. The Ancient Egyptians and Greeks called it the Hercules knot, so it has a long and varied history. It is a very popular knot for necklace and bracelet making. It is more versatile to have a pair of cords in the centre, known as 'lazy' cords.

Flat knot.

Tying the knot

The flat knot consists of two overhand knots: the first is worked left over right, around the lazy cords; and the second is worked right over left, also around the lazy cords.

1. Tie an overhand knot, taking the green cord over the lazy cords and the yellow cord under them.

2. Now tie a second overhand knot, again taking the green cord over the lazy cords and the yellow one under them.

Flat knot choker

The centre of this necklace has a double coin knot, tied with two lengths of blue cord and two lengths of green. The outer two cords of the four on each side of the necklace are used to tie a series of flat knots about the middle two cords. The necklace is closed with a hook and eye fastener.

3. Pull the flat knot tight, then repeat steps 1 and 2.

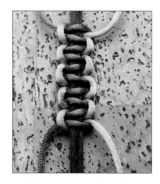

4. Repeat step 3 until the knotting is long enough. The green cord must always be on top of the lazy cords, and the yellow one under them.

You will need

1mm (39in) each of 2mm
blue and green braided cord
2.5m (99in) each of 2mm
blue and green braided cord
Two flat leather crimps
Hook and eye fastener

1. Referring to page 38, tie a double coin knot. Arrange for the short length of each colour to form the lazy centre cords of the flat knots.

2. Now, working on the green side of the necklace and referring to the instructions opposite, tie the first two overhand knots.

3. Tighten the knot, pulling the cords through until the knot is tight up against the double coin knot.

4. Continue tying pairs of overhand knots and tightening them against each other. Keep the tension and knot size the same along the whole length of the necklace.

5. When the necklace is long enough, use one of the outer two cords to make a single button knot around the other three cords (see page 17). Trim and flame seal the working ends. Referring to page 40, secure the leather crimp to the lazy cords, trim and flame seal these, then use the split ring to add the fastener. Repeat steps 2–5 with the blue cords to complete the other side of the necklace.

Plafond knot necklace

The beautiful, handmade fused-glass pendant used for this necklace is complemented by the dark blue satin cord, the neat square plafond knot and the beads and button knots on the sides. A perfect combination! The sliding button knot finish makes it into a variable length necklace, the maximum length of which is 76cm (30in).

You will need

4m (157in) 2mm satin cord

Glass pendant with a channel for the cord to pass through

Six glass beads in matching colours

1. Thread the pendant on to the middle of the cord, then tie a plafond knot with the two ends of cord.

2. Working along each length of cord tie two groups of six button knots with a bead in the middle. Move these groups to leave 3cm (1¼in) lengths of cord between the plafond knot and the start of the first group and the end of this group and the start of the second.

3. Leave a 4cm (1½in) length of cord then tie two more button knots with a bead between them.

4. Equalise the length of cord on each side of the necklace, then tie a sliding button knot on each end.

Opposite

The finished project necklace together with a necklace featuring a lapis bead pendant below a plafond knot. This necklace is also finished with button knots and beads. The earrings are each tied with a plafond knot and a button knot separated by a silver bead. Each earring is decorated with a silver disc from which tiny beads and silver pendants are suspended on seven silver wires.

Celtic Knots

When I moved to Wales and saw Celtic knot designs for the first time, I was fascinated by their flowing curves and repetitive patterns. They had the appeal of a puzzle, which one wants to look at again and again to try and visually follow and even unravel the design. They were to be found illustrating manuscripts, carved in wood and stone, enamelled and etched on to metal, impressed into clay, embroidered on to cushions, batiked and printed on to fabric and even burned as designs in wood. However, it was impossible to find a three-dimensional Celtic knot actually tied with cord or string.

A few years later we moved to Hong Kong. There, to my delight, I discovered Chinese knots, which are very decorative. Tied with a special cord for knotting, they can be combined with beads and are perfect for making jewellery. I learned how to make these knots and have been making and exploring the art of knot-making ever since. Now I have come full circle. Having moved back to Wales, my fascination with Celtic knots has been revived. However, this time I have my experience with other decorative knots to help me create real, three-dimensional Celtic knots.

Did real Celtic knots ever exist in the past? We shall never know, as the cords and string that would have been used to make them would not have survived the passage of time. However, there are many ancient decorative knots in existence which definitely are Celtic in style, being interlaced and plaited in a very similar way. They are very attractive and yet are relatively unknown to artists and teachers in closely allied fibre arts such as weaving, crochet and macramé. They certainly deserve to be revived and used with the colourful cords and beautiful beads that are so readily available today. Until now, these knots could only be found in books and journals for sailors and dedicated knot-tyers. I have searched them out, simplified the descriptions of how to tie them and used them to re-create Celtic knots in three dimensions, which will be perfect for the creation of surprisingly modern, stylish jewellery.

The necklace below (see pages 124–125) combines a Celtic square knot with Celtic beads and a circular pendant.

History

The Celtic civilisation began to flourish more than 2,000 years ago. It is thought to have originated in Central Europe, but its influence spread throughout the continent to Northern Europe. The Celts' artistic sense favoured decoration and pattern over mere representation. Celtic design has a very distinctive style, which has stood the test of time and is as admired today as it was centuries ago. It is typified by its exuberant curves and fluid, finely balanced asymmetrical patterns, stylised leaf and flower patterns and animal motifs, spirals, diagonal key patterns and intricate knotwork and interlacing. Another feature of Celtic artists and craftsmen is the love of strong colours. The ancient Celts were skilled craftsmen, and their artefacts that remain are of excellent quality. Unfortunately, their beliefs and ideas have been lost down the centuries, so what we know of them is mainly through their art and design. Therefore, we have very little mythology to attach to their artwork and the ancient pagan symbolism is almost lost to us. However, the Christian Celts lost no time in adapting the designs and using them to illustrate their own sacred manuscripts.

The designs which interest us for this section are chiefly the interlaced designs developed around the sixth century AD by Christian monks who used the curving, swirling patterns based on the ancient Celtic La Tene period (about 500BC). By the early centuries AD, the Roman Empire had extended into most of Eastern Europe and Roman culture had overtaken that of the Celts in both Central and Eastern Europe. However, Celtic creativity had remained in the more western regions of Europe: the Romans had not reached Ireland or Scotland, and it was here that Celtic art and design survived intact, and the Christian monks were able to use the decorative forms as inspiration for ornamenting their manuscripts.

If you like Celtic knotwork, you are in good company. Famous artists such as Michelangelo, Leonardo da Vinci and Albrecht Durer all used Celtic knot designs in their paintings. Henry VIII has Celtic interlace borders on his cape and sleeves in a portrait by the School of Holbein. It is believed that the wonderfully sinuous Celtic La Tene designs also inspired the Art Nouveau designs of the late nineteenth century.

A Celtic cross from a churchyard in St Fagans, Wales. A wonderful example of the combination of exuberance and control in Celtic knotwork. Note the button knot in the centre.

Celtic interlace and knotwork

Interlaced plaits were also used as decoration by the ancient Egyptians, Greeks and Romans, but these were plain plaits without any modification whatsoever. It was the Christian Celts who devised how to make new patterns from a simple plait by making breaks in the interlacing, and thereby creating more complicated designs. In the construction of patterns, each segment acts as a boundary in which the plait design is contained. It is these boundaries that change the designs from simple plaiting into interlaced knots. It is the boundary, or shape, which we are going to explore in the construction of our Celtic knots in three dimensions.

For readers who are interested in knowing more about the Celts and their art, there are many beautifully illustrated books describing their fascinating history. Interest and appreciation of Celtic art was greatly enhanced in the twentieth century, in fact there has been a modern Celtic revival. In the twenty-first century, the Celtic spirit is a stronger creative force than ever and many talented artists are continuing to produce beautiful work in the Celtic style.

Celtic designs have a magical, mythical quality. The animals are the stuff of legends, with wings and snakes' heads and elaborate, impossibly swirling tails. The plants are so stylised that they could not be identified in any botanical manual. The knots are similarly magical. If a practical knot-tyer examines the illustrations carefully, he or she will find that many of them have pointed loops, and 'floating' spirals and curves, which would never be able to maintain their shapes in three dimensions. This is, of course, part of their beauty, but from a purely practical point of view we will have to get down to basics and use the simpler plaits, braids and interlaced patterns. When adapting the forms, I made a rule for the knots that as far as possible they would be 'self-supporting', in other words they would not need to be attached to anything else to keep their shape (for example, sewn or wired on to a separate piece of fabric). There will be one exception and that is beads! If a bead, pendant or a finding is needed to reinforce the knotting, then all the better, as they will enhance and complement the beauty of the jewellery.

The early Christian Celts would not have used the heart shape, which is a much more recent symbol, but the interlaced pattern is typical of Celtic design.

Tying and tightening Celtic knots

One of the features of Celtic style knots is that the method of weaving the cords gives an alternate 'over and under' pattern. Once you have the knot pattern to follow, the concept is fairly simple. However, the over and under pattern only becomes obvious after you have finished. While you are working on it there are many gaps in the design as the cord changes direction frequently, and this is where it is so easy to go wrong! So, when you are beginning one of the more complicated knots like the heart knot on pages 117–118, make sure you have no distractions and concentrate fully on what you are doing! Once the first cord has completed its pathway, it is easy to add the second or third cords, then you can relax and enjoy weaving the design. Always start the second and third cords in the same place as the first one, otherwise it is impossible to tighten it. Tightening the knot is fairly straightforward as you follow the pathway of the cords to tighten it. You sometimes have to repeat this several times to make the knot as tight as you wish and it has to be done gradually to keep the shape even.

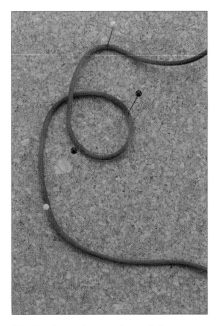

Pinning the cord to a cork mat helps maintain the shape of the knotting.

As the knot starts to take shape, add more pins as needed.

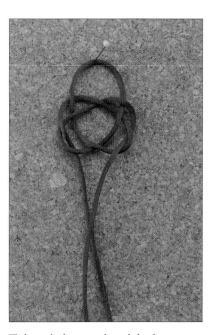

Tighten the knot gently and slowly, removing the pins when necessary.

Braid knot

The pattern of this knot is a basic pattern used frequently in Celtic design, and it is a quick and effective way to make a short, decorative, interwoven braid between beads and button knots. It is much more attractive and stable when the cords are doubled.

You will need

Two pieces of natural cotton cord, 3m (118in) each

Three large and two small painted wooden beads

Fourteen brass hexagonal nuts

Four brass flat washers

Brass hook and eye closure

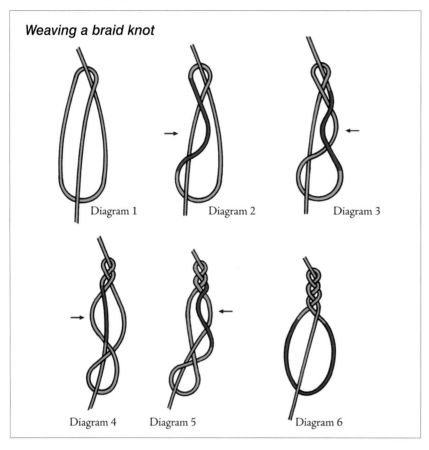

Weaving a braid knot

Diagram 1   Diagram 2   Diagram 3

Diagram 4   Diagram 5   Diagram 6

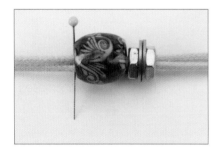

1. Thread two separate cords through a large wooden bead and secure the position with a pin. Thread a brass hexagonal nut, two brass washers and another brass nut on the right-hand side.

2. Use the doubled cord to make a button knot following the instructions on pages 14–16.

3. Tighten the knot partially. The cords should all be parallel, but you may find (as shown above) that they are not. If not, untwist them until they are parallel.

78

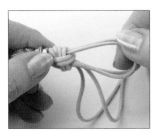

4. Loosen the knot and pull through the loops to move the knot closer to the bead, following the directions on page 16.

5. Your finished knot should look like this.

6. Add brass nuts, beads and button knots as above. Notice that the second and third button knots are smaller as only one cord was used to tie the knot around the other cord – see directions on page 16. Although this knot will not have the space to slide, it is tied in exactly the same way as a sliding button knot.

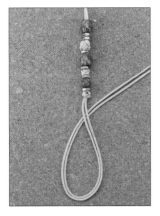

7. Pin the necklace into place on a cork mat and loop with two cords together around and under as shown.

8. Bring the cords down on the right and across to the middle (see diagram 1).

9. Start plaiting using the cords on the left-hand side, by bringing them into the middle (see diagram 2).

10. Take the cord on the right-hand side and bring it to the middle to continue the plait (see diagram 3). Continue plaiting by bringing the cords on the left to the middle as in diagram 4. You will notice that a mirror image of each crossing will form at the bottom of the knot (see diagram 5). These must be uncrossed as you go along.

11. Undo these unwanted crossings by pulling the cords out from the bottom loop and uncrossing the bottom loop as shown in diagram 6.

Tip

When using double cords to make the knot, if you start with the cords entering the knot on the left side, and finish with the cords emerging on the same (left) side, the two looped cords will fall neatly parallel. However, if you start with the cords entering the knot on the left side and finish with them emerging on the opposite (right) side, the looped cords will be twisted and will need to be untwisted throughout the knot.

79

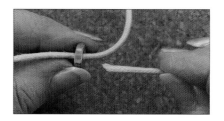

12. When you come to the end of the plait, pull the cord through the loop at the bottom.

13. Ensure all the cords are parallel and flat. Tighten the plait.

14. Make a button knot just after the plait, move it into position and thread a brass nut on.

Tip
Thread one cord through the nut, then flatten it down to thread the other cord through.

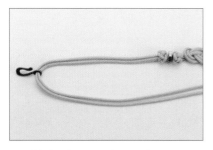

Tip
Alternate which piece of cord you use to make the button knots to ensure the lengths end up the same.

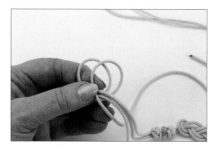

15. Make the next button knot with the longer cord. Thread on the fastener.

16. Make a button knot with one cord around the other three cords (instructions on page 17).

17. Use the longest cord to make another button knot around three cords and trim and seal the ends. Note that two sliding knots have been made side by side – with this thick cord, a double sliding button knot would have been too bulky.

18. Repeat steps 1–16 for the other side to finish the necklace. Ensure that both sides are the same length.

Button and braid necklaces in different styles, both elegant and rustic.

Plaits

Interlaced plaits were used as decoration by the ancient Egyptians, Greeks and Romans as well as the Celts. They are probably one of the most ancient designs in existence. Here I show you how to make a three-stranded plait (also known as King Solomon's plait) and a four-stranded plait which results in a wider braid.

Three-stranded plait

1. Start with three cords, all the same length.

2. Take the right-hand side cord over the middle cord so that it becomes the middle cord.

3. Take the left-hand side cord into the middle.

4. Take the right-hand side cord into the middle.

5. Take the left-hand side cord into the middle.

6. Take the right-hand side cord into the middle.

7. Take the left-hand side cord into the middle.

8. Take the right-hand side cord into the middle.

9. Continue until you have your desired length of plait.

Four-stranded plait

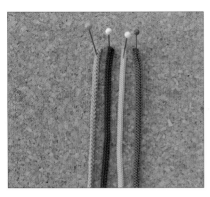

1. Start off with four cords, all of the same length.

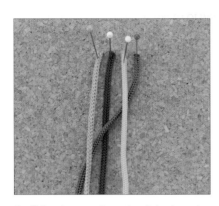

2. Take the cord on the right-hand side underneath the next cord to the left, over the next cord and under the last cord on the far left.

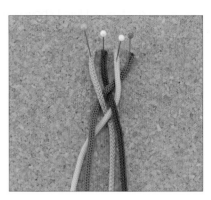

3. Take the cord which is now on the far right (yellow here). Thread it under, then over, and then under the last cord on the left.

4. Take the cord which is now on the far right (deep red here). Thread it under, then over and under the cord on the far left-hand side.

5. Continue until you have your desired length of plait, straightening the plait to keep it vertical as you go along.

Plaited necklace with beads

This plait is an extended King Solomon's knot. It is said that all the wisdom of Solomon is contained in this knot, so the plait must contain even more wisdom! The addition of beads in several colours to complement the colour of the cord makes an interesting pattern when plaited. If you thread one third of the beads on to each strand before you start, it does not take very long to make the necklace.

You will need

2m (78in) 1mm cotton cord

1m (39in) 1mm cotton cord

Approximately 130 small glass beads

One larger bead for the closure

1. Fold the 2m (78in) cord in half to make a loop. With one end of the 1m (39in) length, make two button knots around the folded 2m (78in) cord to create the loop at the end. The longer piece of the 1m (39in) piece of cord makes the third strand of the necklace. Cut off the short end and add a dab of instant glue gel to secure it.

2. Pin the necklace into place and add one third of the beads on to each cord. Leave them on the ends to slide up when needed.

3. Slide each bead up into place before making each crossover. Refer to page 82 if you are unsure of the plaiting method.

4. Continue until the desired length is achieved.

5. Thread the large bead on to two of the cords, bring the ends around and use one of them to make a button knot around the other three (folded) cords and the remaining cord. Tighten the knot and trim the ends. Add a spot of instant glue gel to secure the ends.

You can use a variety of beads to create different effects for your jewellery.

King Solomon's plait necklace

The medieval name for King Solomon's knot is 'the Emblem of Divine Inscrutability', indicating that at that time, knots did indeed symbolise philosophical meanings. The plaited pattern is clearly visible between the beads, and the contrast in the colour of the cord and beads can be very dramatic, yet the method of making the necklace is very simple. It is a delicate design but much stronger than a necklace threaded in the usual way! It is also an economical way of using up beads that are too few in number to make a simple beaded necklace.

You will need

2m (78in) 1mm cotton cord

1m (39in) 1mm cotton cord, same colour

Twenty-one faceted glass beads

Hook and eye closure

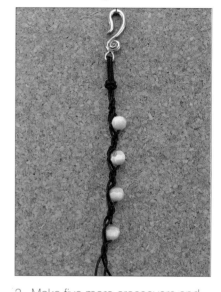

1. Thread the hook closure on to the middle of the 2m (78in) length of cord and fold it in half. Taking the 1m (39in) length of cord, thread one end through the closure for about 6cm (2½in) and use the long end to make a button knot around the other two pieces of cord and the short length. Trim the short end of the cord and secure with instant glue gel.

2. Plait five times (see page 82), then add a bead on the right-hand side cord.

3. Make five more crossovers and add a bead on the right-hand side cord. Continue until you achieve your desired length. You will notice that the beads always fall on the same cord. When you have worked out which cord it is, you can thread the beads on all at once and slide them up as needed.

4. Repeat step 1 for the other end of the necklace, threading on the eye instead of the hook.

Different coloured cords and beads, creating various striking effects.

Four-strand plaited necklace with pendant

The repetition of the plait pattern is reminiscent of the Celtic idea of the ancient rhythm of life, which continues unchanged. Here, leather is used to make the necklace and the plait is wide enough to look attractive with just a pendant to embellish it. It is a good way to use the coloured leather that shops sell already cut into 1m (39in) lengths.

You will need

1.5m (58in) 1.5mm black leather cord

1m (39in) 1.5mm coloured leather cord

Brass hook and eye closure

Pendant (with jump ring to hang it if needed)

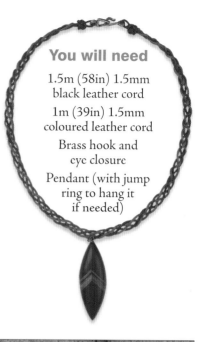

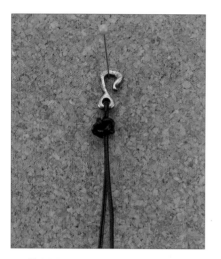

1. Fold the black cord in half, thread the closure on and secure it with a button knot, tying one cord around the other.

2. Fold the coloured length of cord in half and position it underneath the black cord and to the left.

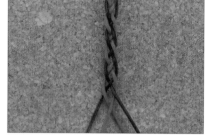

3. Start making a four-stranded plait by bringing the black cord on the right under the coloured cord, over the black and under the coloured on the left (see page 83) and continue until you achieve the desired length.

4. Repeat step 1 for the other end of the necklace, using the eye instead of the hook.

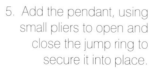

5. Add the pendant, using small pliers to open and close the jump ring to secure it into place.

Opposite

The firmness of the leather complements the design of the plait beautifully.

88

Turk's head knot

This is a very ancient and elegant knot. The continuous pattern of the Turk's head knot was regarded by the Christian Celts as a symbol of connection and continuity for eternity. Its name is believed to have originated from the similarity between this knot and a turban.

You will need

3m (118in) 2mm braided macramé cord

Turk's head bangle

The bangle is made with one single cord which is woven around a cylinder to make nine circuits; three to make the basic plait and six more circuits to treble the plait. It is continuous and the join is invisible on the outside. The knot is constructed around a cardboard cylinder about 7cm (2¾in) in diameter. A larger cylinder may be needed depending on the wrist size. You are actually making a three-stranded plait (see page 82) but because the cord is continuous, you make it with one cord at a time instead of three.

This bangle has three circuits of the cord plaited over and under each other eleven times to make a total of eleven 'scallops' or curves on each side. Generally the number of 'crossovers' depends on the size of the cylinder you are working around. To make the steps clearer here, I have made the knot around a glass so that you can see the back of the knot as well as the front.

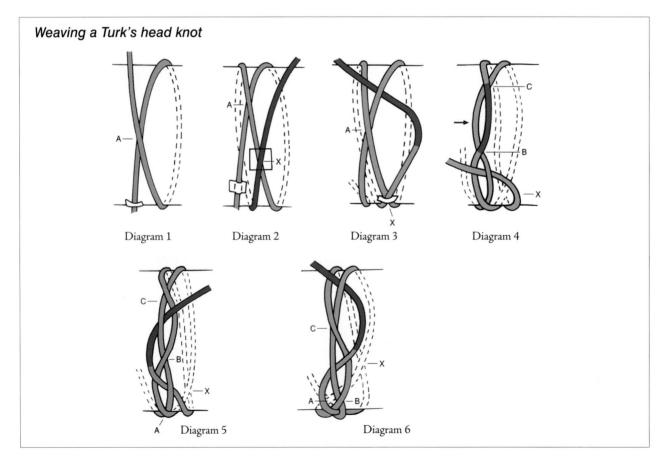

Weaving a Turk's head knot

Diagram 1   Diagram 2   Diagram 3   Diagram 4

Diagram 5   Diagram 6

1. Imagine that the glass in the photograph is a cardboard cylinder. Stiffen the mobile end of the cord (see page 11). Tape the fixed end of the cord to the left side of the cylinder and make one rotation of the cord, crossing at point A (see diagram 1).

2. Make another rotation of the cord and bring it round to the front in between the two cords already there, crossing over the right-hand cord at point X (see diagram 2). Anchor this crossing temporarily using sticky tape (see bottom of diagram 3) as it tends to uncross during plaiting later on.

3. Thread the cord underneath the top cord on the right-hand side, as in diagram 3.

4. Pull the cord through, in between the two cords. Rotate the cylinder towards you, then cross the left-hand fixed cord over the right-hand one (see diagram 4). The new crossing points are shown as B and C.

5. Take the end of the mobile cord and thread it underneath the left-hand cord and over the right-hand cord between B and C (see diagram 5). You can see that the plait is beginning to take shape.

6. Rotate the cylinder slightly towards you, and above crossing C, thread the mobile end under the right-hand cord (see diagram 6).

7. Repeat step 4.

8. Repeat step 5.

9. The cord goes over the right-hand side then above the crossing and underneath the right-hand side cord, as in step 6. Repeat steps 4, 5 and 6 until the desired number of scallops is reached.

Tip

If your cylinder is larger you may need more crossings, but do not make the first plait too tight as you have to double and treble it.

10. By now, you should have reached your starting point. Follow the path through again to make the plait double.

11. Continue following the cord through until you reach the starting point again. Follow the path around again so that the plait is trebled.

12. Bring the cord ends to the inside and trim the ends off, leaving about 1cm (½in) to be glued down.

13. Seal the ends with a thread zapper or a lighter and secure with instant glue gel. Coat the bangle with diluted PVA glue to keep the shape (see step 6 on page 52).

You can make your bangle in any colour you wish; see page 12 for instructions on dyeing cords.

Flat Turk's head pendant

This particular Turk's head knot is very interesting as it has a six pointed star in its centre which is also known as the Seal of Solomon. It is composed of two triangles, one pointing upwards and the other downwards. The upward pointing triangle is a symbol of fire (reaching upwards) and the downward pointing one is the symbol of water (as it flows downwards). When combined, the triangles form a potent symbol of balance and divine union. The flat Turk's head knot makes a lovely pendant, and can also be used to embellish a bangle. In some of the examples I have used acrylic paint to emphasise the star pattern.

You will need

1.2m (47in) 2mm braided macramé cord

Bead or button for centre (optional)

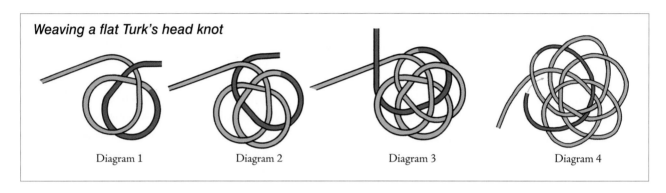

Weaving a flat Turk's head knot

| Diagram 1 | Diagram 2 | Diagram 3 | Diagram 4 |

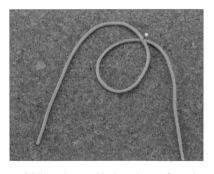

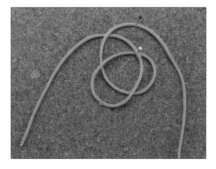

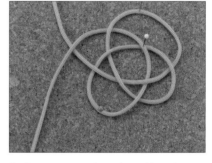

1. Make a loop with the piece of cord and secure with a pin (see diagram 1). Note the second curve goes under the first curve.

2. Loop around and underneath the previous loop to make another loop (see diagram 2).

3. Loop around again, taking the end under, then over, under, over then under the looped cords (see diagram 3).

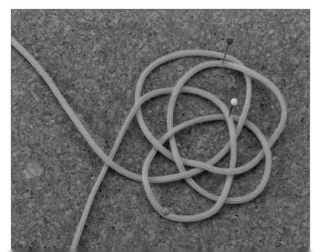

4. Take the cord up and around to create another loop. Take it under, over, under, under, over and under and on top of where the cord started (see diagram 4).

94

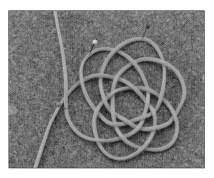

5. Take the cord up and loop around again, taking it under, over, under, over, under, over, under, over and then on top of where the cord started (see diagram 4).

6. Tighten the knot.

7. Follow the path of the cord around again to double the knot. You can either trim and seal the ends or use the ends to create a pendant necklace.

You can also use the flat Turk's head knot to embellish a bangle.

Flat Turk's head knots, some of which are decorated with acrylic paint to emphasise the star shapes.

Turk's head ring

This ring is perfect for lovers as it represents the interweaving of their lives and futures. The method of making it shows how easily this knot can be transformed from a flat knot into a circular one.

You will need

78cm (30in) cord

Tip

Making rings is a marvellous way to use up small ends of cord, though you need at least 52cm (20in) for a double cord ring.

1. Make a bow shape with the cord and pin it in place.

2. Loop around the bottom, over the cord loop and then under the middle piece of cord.

3. Make another loop and then take the cord under the right-hand side and over, then under and over the bottom right-hand side loop.

4. Make a loop at the bottom and follow the same path as where the cord started from.

5. Follow the loops around to double the lead.

6. Follow the path around again for a treble lead ring.

7. The flat shape makes a lovely pendant, but to make a ring, push the centre through towards you.

8. Continue reshaping the knot, tightening the far side of the ring and loosening the centre as you work.

9. Continue until both sides of the ring are parallel. Secure the ends of the cords in the same way as steps 12–13 on page 92.

The finished rings.

5. Take the end of the cord underneath to make the bottom loop of the figure of eight.

6. The cord then passes over the other end of the cord, under the next loop and over to pass back again.

7. The cord then goes over and under the loop on the left-hand side.

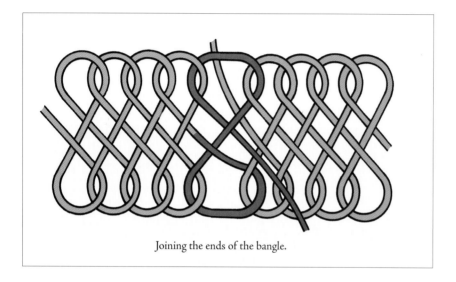

Joining the ends of the bangle.

8. Take the cord under the middle of the figure of eight. Trim and seal the ends using a lighter or thread zapper, and secure them on the inside with instant glue gel as in steps 12 and 13 on page 92. Apply PVA glue to the bangle so that it retains its shape.

Opposite

Use various coloured cords to achieve the effect you want.

Horizontal figure of eight chain

The figure of eight is not so easily recognisable when laid on its side, however, its flowing curves make a very attractive and intricate chain.

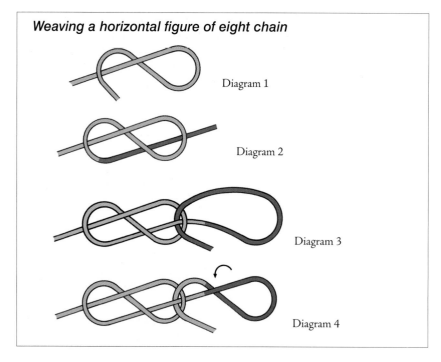

Weaving a horizontal figure of eight chain

Diagram 1

Diagram 2

Diagram 3

Diagram 4

1. Start the chain with a figure of eight on its side.

2. Take the cord up and underneath the 'eight' towards the top right-hand corner.

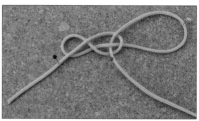

3. Loop around and over, then under and over again.

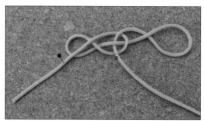

4. Turn the large loop over to form a figure of eight.

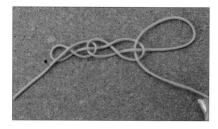

5. Repeat steps 2 and 3, taking the cord end under the loop on the right, then loop back again and then over, under and over again.

6. Repeat steps 4 and 5. When you are satisfied that the chain is the length you want, tuck the free straight cords at the beginning and end through the last loops, as shown in the diagrams.

Horizontal figure of eight chain necklace

This horizontal figure of eight chain works up very quickly. Here I have not added any beads, but a pendant could look very nice with it, as you can see on page 105.

You will need

3m (118in) 2mm cord in a natural beige colour

3m (118in) 2mm cord in turquoise

3m (118in) 2mm cord in deep blue

Brass ring and toggle closure

1. Form the first figure of eight using the turquoise cord, leaving enough cord at the end for a button knot and closures on the left-hand side.

2. Loop backwards over the cord, then under and over again as in step 3 on page 102.

3. Following step 4 on page 102, turn the large loop over and repeat steps 2 and 3. Keep building up the chain, adding knots to form the necklace.

Tip

The necklace can be as short or as long as you want. Keep adding knots until you are happy with the length.

103

4. Add the natural beige cord, leaving a short end at the beginning. This will be threaded through the closure and woven back through the button knot. Follow the path of the turquoise cord, keeping the cords side-by-side. Work the second cord through the length of the necklace.

5. Add in the deep blue cord. Start at the beginning, leaving a long end (this will form the button knot over the turquoise cord). Work the third cord through to the end of the chain.

Tip

The three cord ends will need securing with tape as you move the chain off the cork base. Remove the tape before moving on to step 6.

6. Tuck the free straight cords at the beginning and end of the chain through the last loops. Pass the two blue cords at both ends through the closures after trimming and sealing the beige cord neatly to hide it between the blue cords. Form button knots by working the deep blue cord around the other cords (see page 17). After the button knots are tightened and moved up into the correct place in the design, the ends of the blue cords should be trimmed and sealed neatly.

Opposite

The finished necklace and another example with a pendant. The pendant is secured by weaving the gold cord into the pattern of the necklace, enhancing the design.

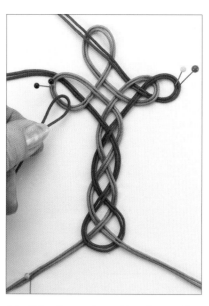

10. Take the rust cords on the left-hand side under the tan cord, over the rust cord and under the tan cord on the right-hand side.

11. Take the rust cord back over the tan cord, under itself, over the tan cord again on the left and under the loop on the left-hand side.

12. Repeat steps 8 and 9 to make the rust loop on the left-hand side. Continue up under the tan loop at the top and over the rust cord, following diagram 2 throughout.

13. Unpin the cross and tighten it. The long rust cords are used to make the rest of the necklace. Trim and secure the tan cords.

14. Add button knots, the gold beads and the closures and secure with sliding double button knots as before.

The finished necklace.

Try different coloured leather cords and beads to create a variety of beautiful cross necklaces.

11. Take the cord over, under and over again.

12. Then under, over and under the top of the top loop, as in diagram 5.

13. Take all the pins out and begin to tighten all the knotwork.

Tip
You will know if you have gone wrong as the cords will spring up when the pins are taken out.

14. Tighten the cords as shown.

15. Add the bead and the earring hook and secure with a button knot, trimming and sealing the ends. Then make the other earring.

The Circle of Life knot is perfect for earrings and also makes a neat brooch (inset).

Triangular knot earrings

This knot is also known as a Triquetra, a Celtic symbol of the Triple Goddess. The triple sign was a common symbol in Celtic myth and legend and the idea of three in one is a possible reason why Christian beliefs such as that of the Trinity were so easily adopted by the Celtic people. The sign represented the three domains of the earth, sea and sky, the trinity of mind, body and soul and many other triple concepts as well.

You will need

Two pieces of 1mm leather cord each 50cm (20in) long

Two earring hooks

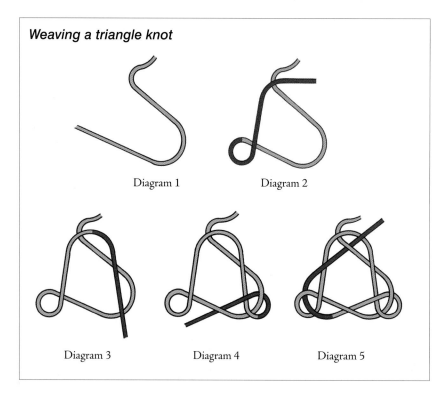

Weaving a triangle knot

Diagram 1   Diagram 2

Diagram 3   Diagram 4   Diagram 5

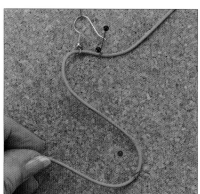

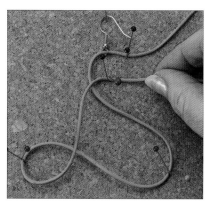

1. Thread the earring hook on to the cord to about halfway and secure it with pins. Make an S-shaped loop as in diagram 1 and pin it in place.

2. Loop around and back up to the top, as in diagram 2.

3. Pin the shape in place.

114

4. Loop back round and down, as in diagram 3.

5. Loop around the outside edge, underneath the outside and over the centre and under the bottom cord, as in diagram 4.

6. Thread the cord through the loop on the left-hand side as shown.

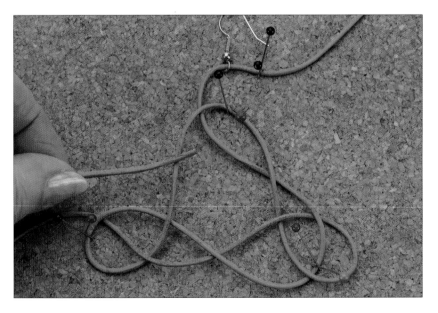

7. Bring the cord back over, near the top of the earring.

9. Go back round to the left and follow the path of the cord again to make the knot double thickness. Trim and secure the ends as shown on page 92.

8. Then under and over again on the right-hand side, as in diagram 5.

Finished triangular knot earrings, incorporating the Celtic symbol of the Triple Goddess.

Two heart brooch

The heart shape is universally considered to be an expression of love. It is a relatively new symbol and would not have been in use in the time of the early Christian Celts. However, its inclusion in the vocabulary of symbolic knotwork shows that Celtic artwork is a living and evolving tradition.

You will need

1.5m (59in) 1mm nylon cord in dark red

Three pieces of 1mm pink nylon cord, each 1.5m (59in) long

Brooch bar

Small piece of thin leather the same size as the brooch bar

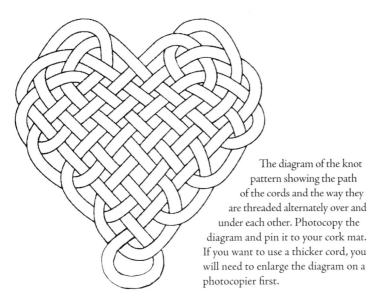

The diagram of the knot pattern showing the path of the cords and the way they are threaded alternately over and under each other. Photocopy the diagram and pin it to your cork mat. If you want to use a thicker cord, you will need to enlarge the diagram on a photocopier first.

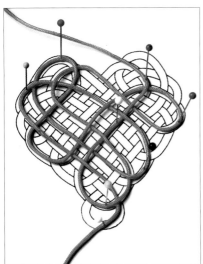

1. Find the middle of the cord and pin it to the centre of the bottom loop on the diagram. Following the guidelines, pin the right half of the cord over or under the crossings as shown on the diagram. Continue until the top of the heart is reached.

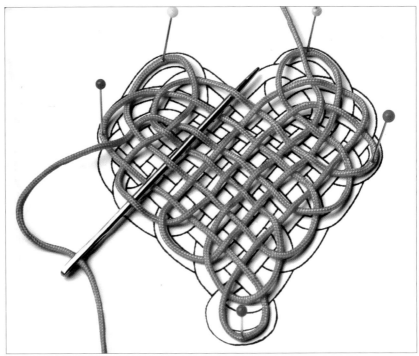

2. Weave the left side of the cord through with a smooth tipped tapestry needle, following the diagram.

117

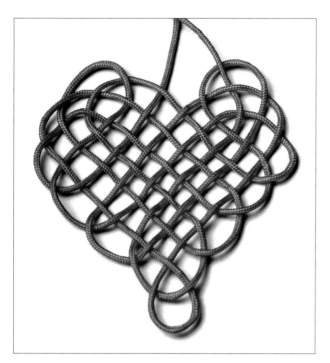

3. When you have completed the heart with one cord, unpin it. Any mistakes will be apparent, as the cord will spring up.

4. Weave in the second cord, following the lead of the first cord, starting at the bottom and using the tapestry needle as before.

5. Tighten all the cords as shown above. Make another heart knot using only pink cord and following the steps shown above.

6. Trim and secure the end of the cords neatly using instant glue gel. Glue the brooch pin to a small thin piece of leather and then stick this on to the two-tone heart with instant glue gel. Attach the pink heart to the first heart using small spots of instant glue gel.

You can use the heart knot to make a variety of jewellery.

Josephine knot necklace

This is an ancient Celtic knot that has been popular for thousands of years. It can be found in various cultures, each of which has a different name for the knot. Josephine is a relatively recent name, after Napoleon Bonaparte's Empress. Since there is ample evidence that early Celtic society was matriarchal, it is appropriate to use the name here. In this necklace the knots are linked from side to side and made using just one continuous cord – an unusual style and very attractive. The beaded scallops stabilise the necklace design.

You will need

4m (160in) 2mm black cotton cord

1.5m (59in) 1mm black cotton cord

130 assorted colour glass beads

Hook and eye closure

Weaving a Josephine knot

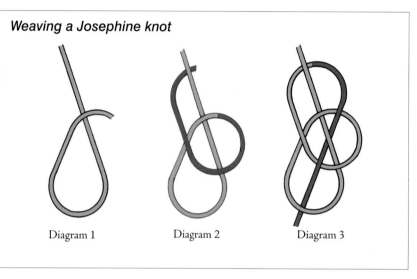

Diagram 1   Diagram 2   Diagram 3

1. Make a loop with the 2mm cotton cord (see diagram 1) and pin it in place.

2. Make another loop on top, and slightly to the right (see diagram 2).

3. Cross the cord over and then under as shown.

120

4. Loop around and over, then under, over and under.

5. Pull the cord through so the knot takes shape as above (see diagram 3). Repeat steps 1–5 to make another knot below the first one. Continue until you have made about twelve knots.

6. Take the length of thinner cord and tie a larkshead knot (shown above) to the top Josephine knot in the necklace.

7. Add about nine beads to the short end of the thin cord and pin it in place as shown.

8. Add about eleven beads to the next scallop and loop through the next Josephine knot as shown to begin another larkshead knot.

121

10. Bring the cord underneath the loop to finish the larkshead knot. Continue until you have added beaded scallops to each Josephine knot, adding eleven beads each time.

9. Loop the thinner cord through the Josephine knot again.

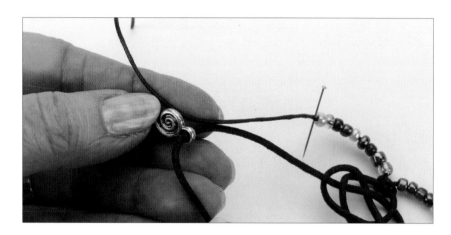

11. Add nine beads to the end of the thinner cord after the last larkshead knot. Secure them with a pin as shown. Thread the closure on to the thicker piece of cord.

12. With the end of the thicker cord, make a button knot around the thin cord and the two cords to secure. Tighten the button knot, then cut and secure the thin cord with instant glue gel to stop it slipping out.

13. Repeat steps 11 and 12 for the other end of the necklace, using the hook fastener instead of the eye.

Jospehine knots create intricate patterns, perfect for necklaces and bracelets. The necklace and bracelet in black and the blue necklace with the turquoise pendant were also made with Josephine knots, but the series of knots were made in the more traditional vertical style, starting with the cord folded in half, and the knots made with the two cord ends, one on each side.

Celtic square knot necklace

To the monks of early Christianity, the square symbolised the creation of the manifold universe. They used the geometric method of construction to create knots to fill squares in their designs for embellishing manuscripts. This knot fits into a square, although here we have adapted it to make a necklace with a pendant so the shape has become slightly elongated. Knots made with cord (compared to knots constructed geometrically on paper) have a life of their own!

You will need

3m (118in) silver-coloured 2mm satin cord

3m (118in) turquoise 2mm braided cord

One Celtic silver circular pendant

Two Celtic spangle hexagonal silver beads

Six Celtic oval silver beads

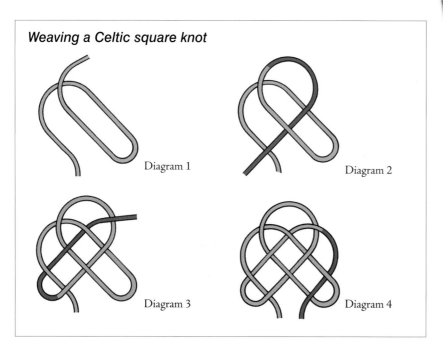

Weaving a Celtic square knot

Diagram 1

Diagram 2

Diagram 3

Diagram 4

1. Find the middle of the silver cord and fold the cord in half at this point. Tie a larkshead knot around the Celtic pendant.

2. Make a loop with the cord on the left-hand side (see diagram 1).

3. Take the right-hand side cord and thread it over, under and over the other cord (see diagram 2).

4. Loop the cord around, taking it up and under, over then under (see diagram 3).

5. Loop the cord around the top, take it under and then over, following diagram 4. Tidy the knot, making sure it is symmetrical.

6. Find the middle of the turquoise cord, pin it in place as shown and start to follow the path of the silver cord around again.

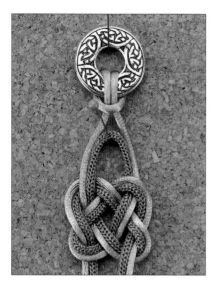

7. Finish following the path of the first knot with the turquoise cord.

8. Make a button knot with the silver cord around the other three cords. Then make two button knots further down with the turquoise cord.

9. Continue adding beads and knots as shown.

10. Finish with two sliding double button knots.

The finished necklace.

Using the basic square knot, experiment to create your own designs.

Rectangular Celtic knot necklace

The rectangular knot is just an extended square knot and this knot is constructed of several Josephine knots intertwined one after the other. If the pattern is extended even further it would become a Josephine knot border, another example of the versatility of Celtic knots. Here the knot combines beautifully with a silver pendant.

You will need

3m (118in) light red 2mm satin cord

3m (118in) dark red 2mm satin cord

Large silver pendant

Two Celtic spangle (hexagonal) silver beads

Four Celtic lozenge silver beads

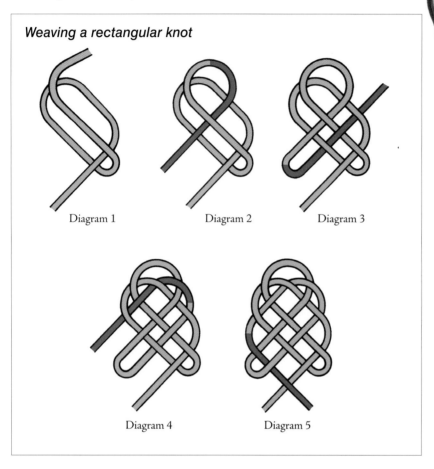

Weaving a rectangular knot

Diagram 1

Diagram 2

Diagram 3

Diagram 4

Diagram 5

1. Thread the cords through the pendant loop until the pendant is halfway along. Loop the light red cord and pin into place.

2. Loop the cord around, under and through as in diagram 1.

3. Take the light red cord on the right-hand side, loop it around and pin it into place, over, under and over the first loops, as in diagram 2.

4. Loop down, around and underneath, then over and under towards the top right as shown (see diagram 3).

5. Loop around the top, over the cord, under, over and under and through to the other side (see diagram 4). I have moved the black pin to secure the loop in place.

6. Bring the cord down, over then under and through to the bottom, laying it over the other cord (see diagram 5).

7. Follow the path of the light red cord with the dark red cord.

129

Ornamental Knots

Sometimes I think that I have not chosen knots, but that they have chosen me! Ever since I saw my first ornamental knot I have been utterly fascinated by their individuality: they are small and self-contained, they are handmade without the need for elaborate equipment, and their intricate patterns have an air of confidence and self-importance which I find very beguiling. They have a fascinating history and folklore all of their own. When I discover a new knot that I like, it does not leave me in peace until I have learned how to make it and combine it with beads to create a lovely piece of jewellery. Carefully chosen knots and beads can enhance each other beautifully!

Knots are as old as mankind. As man migrated across the world and travelled ceaselessly from place to place, he took his knots and knotting skills with him. Chinese knots and Celtic knots are the two main types of purely ornamental knots that have never had any simple useful function except to be beautiful and decorative, and perhaps to adorn other items.

Sailors used practical knots for many purposes aboard ship, but in their spare time the only thing they had available to them was rope and string, so, as well as tying functional knots, they used them to create very attractive decorative knots. They called them 'fancy knots', and this section shows you in detail how to make various styles of knots, including fancy knots, and how to combine them with beads and pendants to make very unusual and stylish jewellery.

Many of the same knots can be found in different cultures with a different name in each because there have been a lot of cross-cultural exchanges. The best known one is the macramé knot called the Josephine knot, also called the double coin knot by the Chinese, and known as the Carrick bend by sailors. There are other knots, too numerous to list here, that are known by several different names.

It is interesting to note that both the Chinese and the ancient Celts used knots to represent exactly the same aspects of life and nature, such as the continuity and eternal cycle of life; the contrasts of dark and light, winter and summer, male and female; the concept of balance and harmony; and the interconnection of all things in the natural world. You can find out more about the history and folklore of the different Chinese and Celitc decorative knots, in more detail, in the previous sections.

Opposite

Lampwork beads by Rachelle Goldreich on a necklace of macramé square knots and spiral knots.

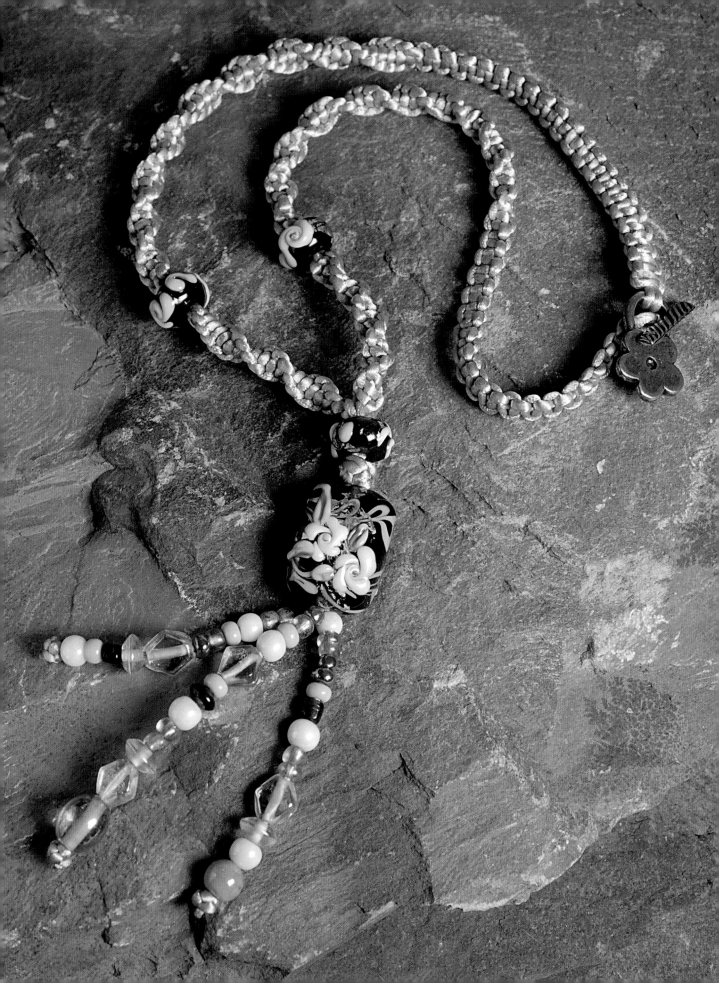

Pineapple knot

The pineapple knot is an extended button knot, and is also called an extended diamond knot, but pineapple knot sounds much nicer!

This knot will be easier to follow if you are already familiar with making the button knot. It looks difficult at first, but once you have made one or two the method will begin to make more sense to you.
It is made with the two ends of the cord as if they are separate cords.

The tightening differs from the button knot: instead of simply pulling the loops through around the knot, you also work up and down the knot as you pull the loops through, and tighten each end of the cord separately.

You will need

One toggle clasp

2.5m (98in) 2mm satin cord

Celtic beads: two star-shaped, two 'Cyfrin dragon's eye', two 'Cyfrin balls', one large ball and one square

Pineapple knot bracelet

The knot looks very attractive and interesting when combined with beads, as you can see in this bracelet.

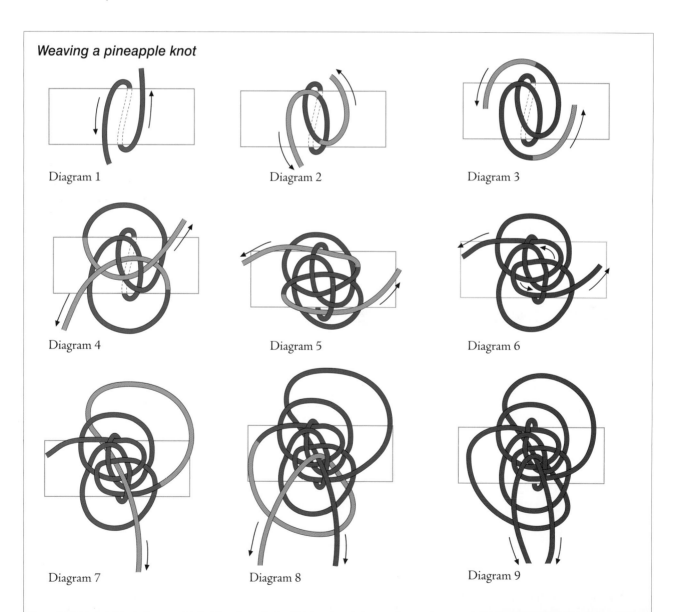

Weaving a pineapple knot

Diagram 1

Diagram 2

Diagram 3

Diagram 4

Diagram 5

Diagram 6

Diagram 7

Diagram 8

Diagram 9

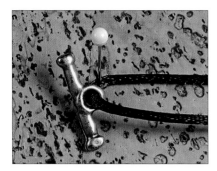

1. Thread the toggle to the middle of the cord and pin the cord in place on the corkboard.

2. Cut a piece of card 12 x 4cm (4¾ x 1½in) and pin it on top of the cord close to the toggle. Take one end of the cord upwards and the other end downwards.

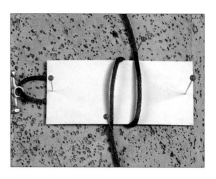

3. Fold the ends of the cords over the card and pin them as shown (see diagram 1).

4. Remove the pins, overlay the cords as shown and repin. (see diagram 2).

5. Spiral the cords once around the new pins and pin each in place halfway up the card. (see diagram 3).

6. Take the end on the right, take it over the first two cords to its left, under the third and over the fourth as shown.

7. Mirror the action with the other end of the cord, taking it over two cords to its right, under the third and over the fourth (see diagram 4).

8. Take the same end back from right to left through the middle loop at the top as shown (it is the loop that appears from under the white card).

9. Carefully pull the cord through to make a loop at the top right.

135

10. Mirror the action with the other end of the cord, threading it from the left to right (see diagram 5).

11. Pull both cords slightly tighter to make the shape shown above (see diagram 6).

12. Take the free end that is now on the right and loop it round the top of the knot, before taking it under all of the cords and bringing it up in the central hole. Pull the cord down over the rest of the cords (see inset and diagram 7).

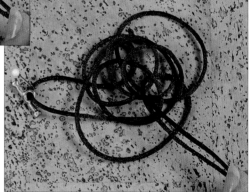

13. Mirror the process with the other free end, taking it down and round to the right then under the cords, up through the centre and upwards over the other cords (see diagram 8).

14. Take hold of both free ends and take them downwards. Carefully remove all of the pins except the one holding the toggle in place (see diagram 9).

15. Carefully slide the card out from the knot.

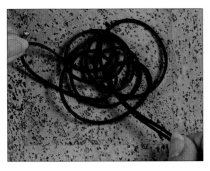

16. Remove the last pin, pick up the middle of the cord with your left hand, just below the toggle, and take the free ends in your right hand.

17. Gently pull your hands apart to begin to form the knot.

18. Starting with the largest loose loop, even out the tension through the knot by working up and down the knot until it looks like this. This is a tightened pineapple knot.

19. When the knot has taken shape, move it up towards the toggle in the centre of the cord in the same way as the button knot (see page 16).

20. Thread a star-shaped bead on to both ends of the cord and move it up to the pineapple knot.

21. Secure the bead in place by making a second pineapple knot in the same way as the first and tightening it next to the bead.

22. Put a Cyfrin ball bead inside a Cyfrin dragon's eye bead. Treating this as one bead, thread it on the ends of the cord, move it up adjacent to the second pineapple knot, then secure it in place with a third pineapple knot.

23. Repeat this process with a square bead, a second two-part bead, a second star bead and a large ball bead, separating and securing them with pineapple knots.

Tip
You can add another bead and knot if you want a longer bracelet.

137

24. Make a loose pineapple knot next to the final round bead (inset), then take one end of the cord through the toggle loop. Take the other end through the loop in the other direction. This makes the cords much less likely to loosen.

25. Pull the ends through until the toggle loop is near the loose knot, then feed one end into and through the knot.

26. Feed the other end through the knot, then pull both ends tight. Tighten the knot around the cords. Secure the ends where they leave the knot with a spot of instant glue gel.

27. Trim and seal the ends of the cords to finish the bracelet.

Opposite:

This knot works really well for necklaces, as shown by the three variations here. The top left variation uses lampwork beads made by Ray Skene, while the Celtic beads on the project bracelet are from Black Dragon's range. The necklace on the top right uses Greek clay beads and gold beads from Black Dragon, while the lower right necklace uses porcelain beads and Greek clay beads.

139

Chain knot

Phoenix tail necklace

This necklace is made of chain knots, made with two cords instead of the more usual one. This makes it much more stable and attractive. A pendant which is stunning on its own does not need the addition of a lot of knots, as they could detract from its appearance. The phoenix tail is beautiful but subtle, and will complement virtually any pendant.

Here I use a beautiful pendant in lapis lazuli and silver made by Native Americans, from Santa Fe, New Mexico.

I like the chain when made with two cords of the same colour, but it can also be made with two different colours. This has the advantage that it shows off the construction of the chain very nicely, and it is a great way to make a cord of the necklace the focal point.

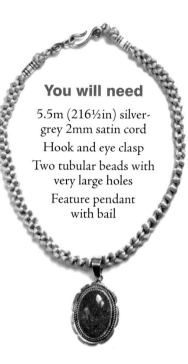

You will need

5.5m (216½in) silver-grey 2mm satin cord

Hook and eye clasp

Two tubular beads with very large holes

Feature pendant with bail

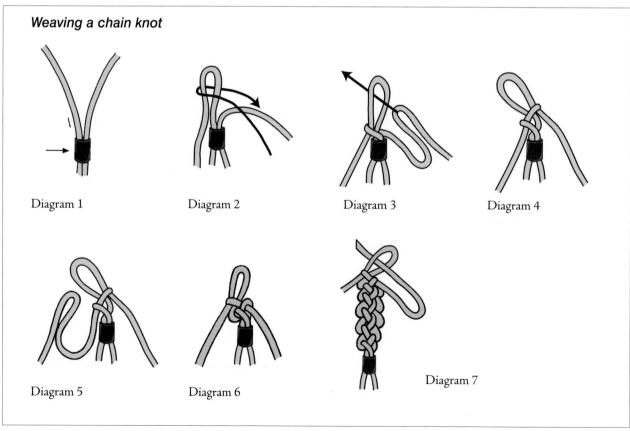

Weaving a chain knot

Diagram 1

Diagram 2

Diagram 3

Diagram 4

Diagram 5

Diagram 6

Diagram 7

140

1. Find the centre point of your cord, thread the hook and run it down the cord to this point.

2. Make a button knot around the cord next to the hook, following the instructions on pages 17 and the diagrams on page 14.

3. Put both of the ends of the cord through a tubular bead and run it up to the knot.

4. Make a loop with the cord on the left-hand side. Hold the loop next to the bead with your left hand as shown.

5. Take the end of the cord on the right and wrap it round the loop (see diagram 2).

6. Hold the wrapped part tightly and make a second loop with the cord on the right-hand side.

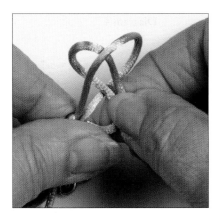

7. Take the new loop through the first loop from front to back (see diagram 3).

8. Gently pull the first loop closed around the second loop (see diagram 4).

141

9. Ease the resultant knot tight.

10. Make a third loop with the cord on the left (see diagram 5).

11. Take the third loop through the second loop from front to back (see diagram 6).

12. Pull the second loop closed around the third loop.

13. Make a fourth loop with the cord on the right, take it through the third and pull the third loop tight. You can now see the chain knot pattern start to emerge.

14. Continue working chain knots until the work measures 32cm (12½in). Leave a loop at the end.

Detail of chain knots.

15. Take the right-hand end of the cord through the loop (see diagram 7).

16. Pull the loop tight around the cord. (Note: if your pendant has a small bail or loop, add it on to the chain at this point.)

17. Thread a tubular bead with both ends of the cord and run it down to the end of the chain knots.

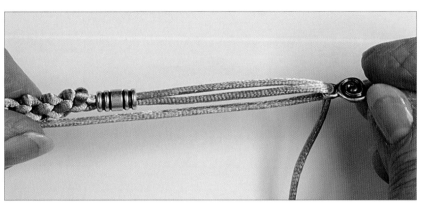

18. Thread the eye of the clasp on to the ends and run it down to approximately 10cm (4in) from the bead to allow space for tying a button knot.

19. Use your left hand to hold one free end of the cord parallel with the cords leading from the knot.

20. Use the free end to tie a button knot around the other three cords.

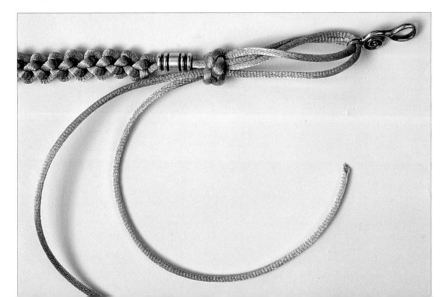

Note
Instructions for tying a button knot around other cords can be found on pages 17–18.

Tip
If you are right-handed, you will find it easier to turn the work from right to left before tying the knot.

143

21. Pull the extra cord through after moving the knot next to the bead.

22. Trim and seal the ends of the cord. Add an invisible spot of instant glue gel if needed.

23. Slip the bail and pendant on to the eye end of the cord and run it down to the central point to finish the necklace.

Opposite

Try different colours to complement your feature pendant best. Clockwise from top left: turquoise and silver, black and gold porcelain, enamelled Gustav Klimt-inspired pendant, and the project necklace with blue lapis lazuli and silver. In the centre a fantasy water nymph bead by Rachelle Goldreich makes a beautiful pendant.

Guinevere knot

Guinevere's necklace

This lovely knot has inspired quite a number of people to start making Celtic knots. I received the design from Todd and Sherry Greer in Austin, Texas, in the United States, who make hand-tied Celtic knotwork. They learned this knot from Dave Love at a Renaissance fair.

Another name for the Guinevere knot could be the 'Renaissance knot' as it keeps reappearing, tied in leather and different cords. It is great to know that so many people are now tying Celtic knots and making jewellery with them.

You will need

3m (118in) light red
2mm satin cord

3m (118in) dark red
2mm satin cord

One pendant with bail

Celtic beads: four bars and
two 'Cyfrin dragon's eye'

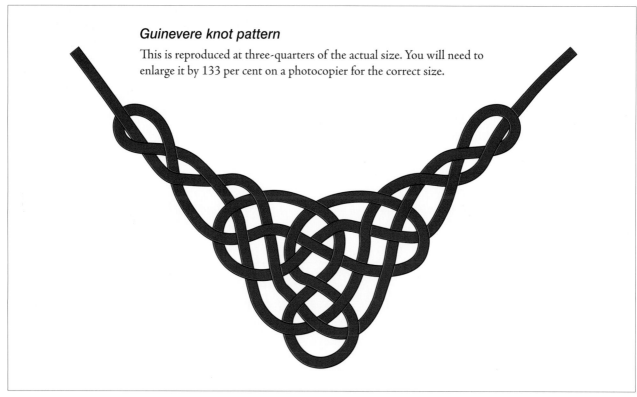

Guinevere knot pattern

This is reproduced at three-quarters of the actual size. You will need to enlarge it by 133 per cent on a photocopier for the correct size.

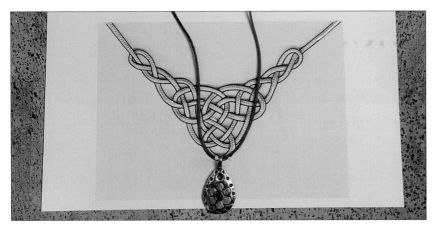

1. Photocopy the pattern and pin it to your cork mat. Thread the pendant on to the middle of the light red cord and pin it in place on either side of the pendant.

Tip

You can enlarge the pattern on a photocopier if you wish.

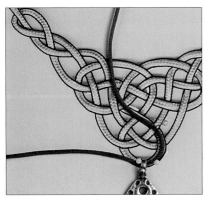

2. Starting with the end of the cord emerging from the right of the pendant, begin to lay the cord so that it follows where the pattern leads. Pin where necessary to keep the cord on the pattern.

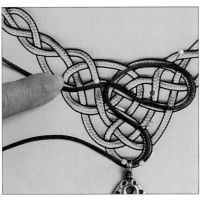

3. Continue laying the cord along the lines of the pattern. Where the pattern leads the cord back on itself, check whether the pattern indicates you to take the cord under or over itself to continue.

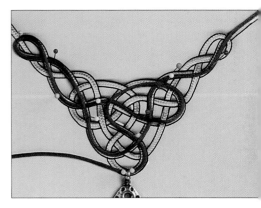

4. Work carefully around the pattern, making sure the cord goes under and over itself where appropriate. The pattern eventually leads the right-hand cord off to the top right corner. Secure it with a pin.

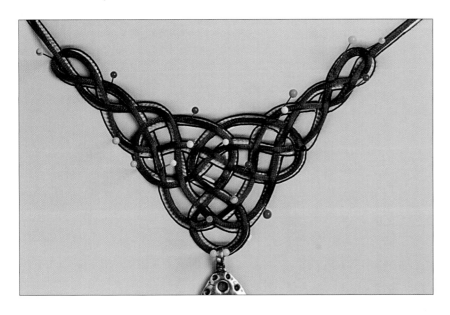

5. Follow the pattern in the other direction using the cord emerging from the left of the pendant. Pay careful attention to the 'unders and overs' where the cords cross each other.

147

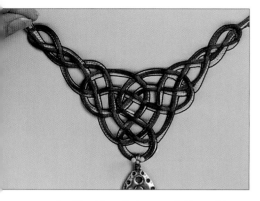

Note

At this point, if the weaving is correct, the knot will be stable. If not, one piece of the design will spring up and loosen, so check that the overs and unders in the weaving are correct. If not, undo it and re-weave the cord.

6. The triangle is now fairly stable, so you can remove most of the pins. If you feel the work moves too much, you can add a couple of extra pins to support it.

7. Thread the dark red cord on to the pendant and run it through until the central point of the cord is in the pendant. Pin it to secure it in place within the loop of the light red cord at the bottom.

8. Follow the pattern again, laying the right-hand end of the dark red cord down next to the light red cord. Make sure that the cords remain touching, but do not allow them to cross. When the cord reaches the top right corner, pin the cord to secure it in place.

9. Lay the left-hand end of the dark red cord down in the same way and pin it at the top left.

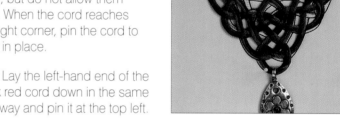

10. Remove all but the pin next to the pendant and begin tightening the knot by pulling the loops away from the central point. Do not try to tighten too much at once as this can distort the shape.

11. Continue pulling the cords around the pattern, following the path in which the cords were laid down. Do not allow the light red and dark cords to cross at any point: keep them next to one another.

12. Notice how tightening enlarges a loop, which is then tightened by pulling it a short distance further along the design. This gradual process keeps everything aligned in the correct shape.

13. The piece will gradually get smaller as you tighten, so a stage-by-stage approach is best. Work around and around the cord until the knot is roughly half the size of the original pattern.

14. Remove the piece from the cork mat and pattern, then tie a button knot around the light red cord on the top left using the adjacent dark red cord.

15. Thread a bar bead on to both cords, slide it down to the button knot, then make a second button knot next to the bead with the light red cord knotted around the dark red cord.

16. Thread both cords through one side of a Cyfrin dragon's eye bead (see inset), then run it down to the second button knot. Make a third button knot by tying the light red cord around the dark red cord and move it down within the dragon's eye bead. Take the ends of the cords out of the other side of the bead. (See page 14 for how to move the button knot.)

17. Make a button knot above the bead using the light red cord around the dark red cord. Slip on a bar bead and then tie a sliding button knot using the dark red cord around the light red cord.

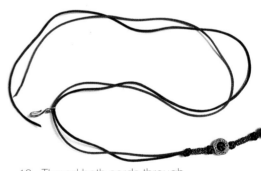

18. Thread both cords through the hook and run it down to approximately 15cm (6in) from the last button knot.

Note

It is important to use – and alternate – both coloured cords to make the knots. If you use only one colour the knots will slide up and down and spoil the design.

149

19. Using the free end of the light red cord, tie a sliding button knot around the other three cords. Move the knot up to the hook and then tighten.

20. Cut and seal the end of the light red cord.

21. Tie a sliding button knot around the other three cords using the free end of the dark red cord. Move the knot up to the hook and then tighten it. Cut and seal the dark red cord. You now have two sliding knots side by side which is more comfortable than a double button knot on the back of the neck. When moving them, hold both at the same time as if they were one.

22. Repeat this process using the cords on the right-hand side of the piece, substituting an eye for the hook when finishing.

Note

When there is a clasp in between the sliding knots, each sliding knot must be moved separately to adjust the length of the necklace.

Both can be moved at once if there is no clasp in between them.

Opposite:

The finished necklace is at the bottom right. The blue necklace to the left is made with a thick firm cord which keeps stable once knotted even though it is only a single cord, while the gold necklace uses leather cords and has a feature lampwork bead by Rachelle Goldreich.

Epaulette knot

Epaulette knot bracelet

Traditionally an epaulette knot is a decoration worn on the shoulder of certain uniforms, especially military ones. However it also looks very good made with leather cord and combined with beads as you see in the bracelet here.

It is based on the Josephine knot (see page 13) extended on each side. Pay particular attention to the 'unders and overs' at the beginning as they do vary a little from the basic Josephine knot. Here the first leather cord starts at the top of the central knot and the second cord starts at the bottom of the knot. It is more difficult to tighten the knot as each cord goes in a different direction… but the results are well worth the effort!

You will need

Two 2m (79in) lengths of black 1mm leather cord

Four dichroic fused glass beads with parallel holes

One silver toggle clasp

Note

Any beads with two parallel holes (or even those with one central hole) will work with this method.

Weaving an epaulette knot

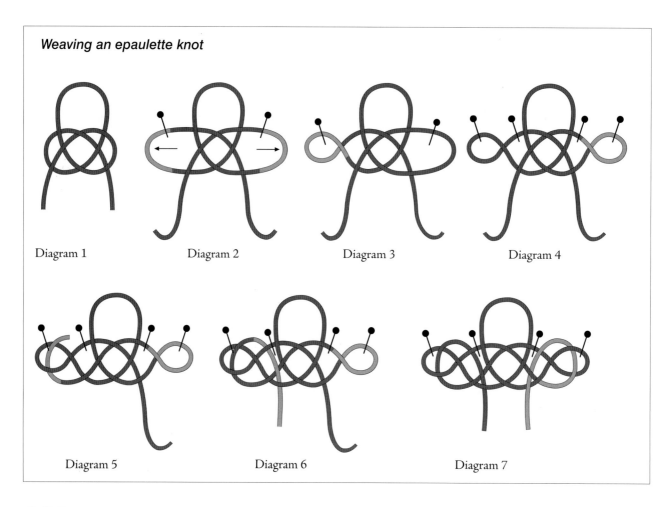

Diagram 1

Diagram 2

Diagram 3

Diagram 4

Diagram 5

Diagram 6

Diagram 7

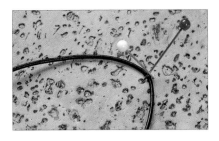

1. Find the centre of the first piece of leather cord and place it on the cork mat. Hold it in place with two pins crossed as shown so that the pins can not damage the leather.

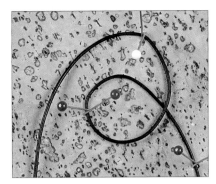

2. Make a loop with the right-hand end of the cord with the free end going underneath and pin it as shown in step 1.

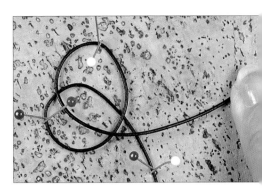

3. Take the left-hand end of the cord over the loop.

Note

It is extremely important that the lace goes over and under the correct parts of the cord when the knot is woven. Make frequent references to the diagrams to make sure that each stage is correct.

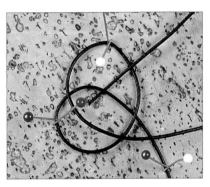

4. Take the left-hand end (which is now on the right-hand side) up to the right then down and weave it over and under the cord as shown.

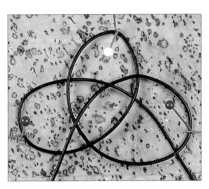

5. Take the cord over and off to the left to make the shape shown. See diagram 1. Note that the unders and overs vary from the basic Josephine knot (see page 13).

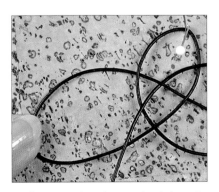

6. Remove the pins on the left and ease the loop out (see diagram 2).

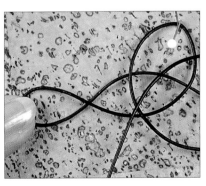

7. Twist the left loop up and over itself (see diagram 3).

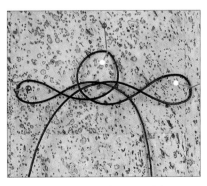

8. Pin the loop in place and then twist the loop on the right-hand side down and over itself (see diagram 4).

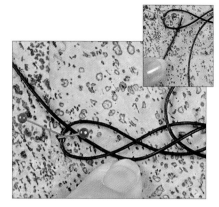

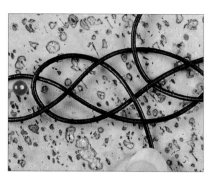

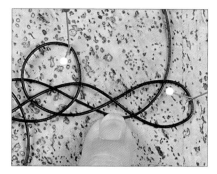

9. Take the left-hand end of the cord under the left-hand twisted loop (see inset). Pull the end through to the top left while holding the cord in place as shown in the main photograph (see diagram 5).

10. Take the end under, over and under the cord as shown to lock the leather in position on the left (see diagram 6).

11. Take the right-hand end over and through the rightmost loop, as shown; working the opposite overs and unders to the side you have completed. Remember to hold the cord in place.

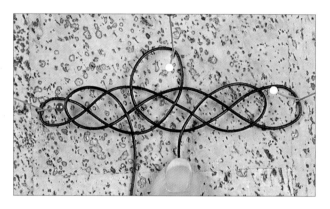

12. Take the end over, under and over the cord as shown to lock the leather (see diagram 7). This completes an epaulette knot.

13. Starting from the middle of the knot, gradually work around the cord, tightening it.

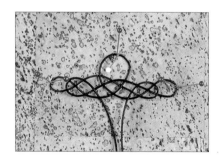

14. Continue tightening the knot until it measures roughly 5cm (2in).

Note

When tightening, remember to work in short stages, gradually making the knot as a whole smaller and tighter.

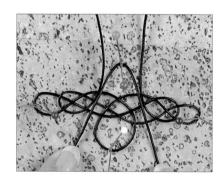

15. Turn your cork mat around and pin the second length of leather on the mat as shown. Starting at what is now the top of the knot will ensure that the second cord will start and end in the opposite direction to the first one.

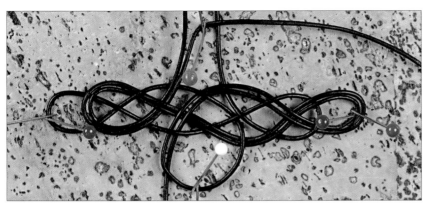

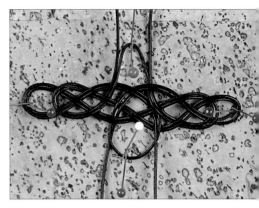

16. Following the path of the first length of cord, weave the left-hand end of the new cord around the knot.

17. Weave the right-hand end of the new length around the knot, following the path of the first knot.

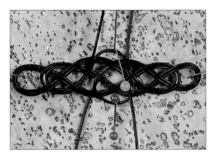

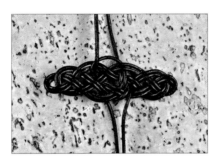

18. Gradually tighten the knot. Because there are two cords going in opposite directions, tighten each cord simultaneously at each point by pulling one cord in one direction and the other in the opposite direction. This is painstaking but worth the effort.

19. Continue tightening until the work is roughly half its original size. Remove the pins as necessary while you are tightening the knot. This completes a double epaulette knot.

20. Thread one of the beads on to the leather cords below the knot.

21. Carefully anchor the double knot and bead with a pin or two, then make a single epaulette knot below the bead.

22. Tighten the knot, then slip a second bead on to the ends of the cord.

23. Make a third epaulette knot and tighten it a little more than the previous knot to ensure it is smaller.

Firecracker knot

Firecracker knot earrings

Firecrackers in China are believed to frighten away evil spirits. I first saw these knots in many different colours in an elaborate Chinese decorative hanging, combined with a fearsome lion dog's head and several different Chinese knots. When the ends are left free they make a lovely tassel, known as the Tassel of Good Fortune, and make elegant earrings.

The firecracker knot is also known as a crown knot, and one single knot (as in diagram 4, below) is known as a Japanese bend.

You will need

Ten 60cm (24in) lengths of gold 1mm satin cord

Two feature beads

A pair of earring hooks

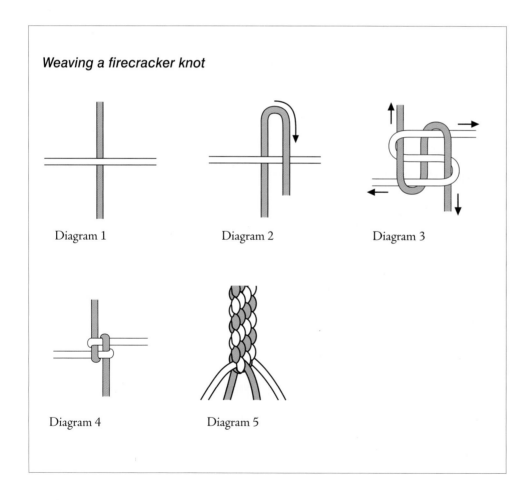

Weaving a firecracker knot

Diagram 1

Diagram 2

Diagram 3

Diagram 4

Diagram 5

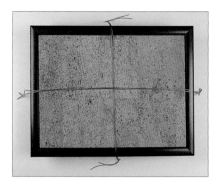

1. Take two lengths of gold cord and lay them vertically across your cork mat. Lay another pair of gold cords horizontally to make a cross (see diagram 1).

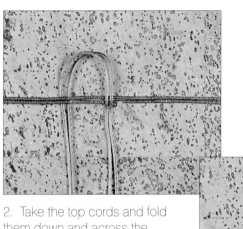

2. Take the top cords and fold them down and across the right-hand pair of cords to make a loop (see diagram 2).

3. Take the right-hand cords and fold them across the cords at the bottom, making a loop on the right side.

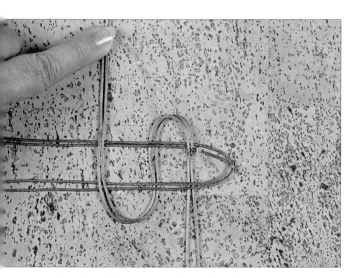

4. Take the left-hand pair of cords at the bottom, and fold them across the cords at the left.

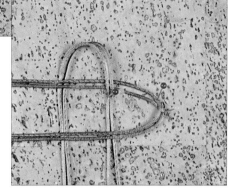

5. Take the upper pair of cords on the left and fold them across the pair currently pointing upwards, then take them over and through the loop as shown (see diagram 3).

159

15. Trim and seal the loose ends of the cord coming from the button knot.

16. Make a tube by rolling up a 3.5 x 6cm (1½ x 2½in) piece of plastic acetate. Secure it with a small piece of sticky tape.

17. Dampen the tassel, slip it inside the tube and allow to dry.

18. Run the tube down the tassel to the length desired, then use it as a guide to cut the tassel to length.

19. Make a second earring in the same way.

Pink and white 'Kimono' glass beads
made by Rachelle Goldreich were
used in both the necklace and the pink
earrings, while I used blue-white and
gold lampwork beads for the project.
These were also made by Rachelle.

Pipa knot

Pipa knot earrings

A pipa is a Chinese string instrument rather like a lute. This knot is named after the pipa as it has the same shape. The shape also gives it the alternative name 'teardrop knot'.

Take your pick of which name you like better! Whatever you call it, this knot has a lovely graceful shape and is particularly good for earrings.

You will need

Two 60cm (24in) lengths of turquoise 1mm leather cord

Two 50cm (20in) lengths of turquoise 1mm satin cord

A pair of earring hooks

Two large and four small beads

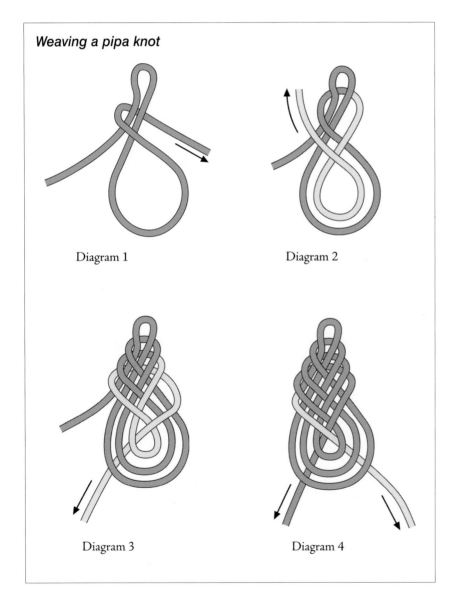

Weaving a pipa knot

Diagram 1

Diagram 2

Diagram 3

Diagram 4

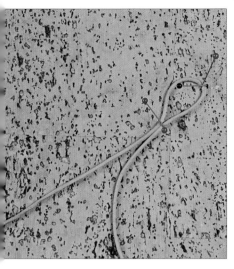

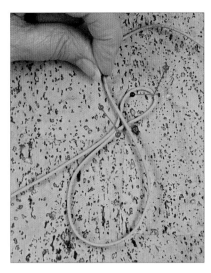

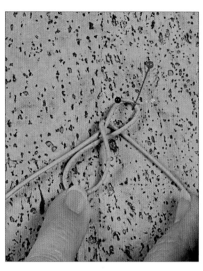

1. Secure the 60cm (24in) leather cord to the cork mat. Pin either side of the leather as shown to avoid spoiling it. Curl the leather round into an uncrossed loop, leaving a 10cm (4in) tail on the left-hand end.

2. Bring the right-hand end of the cord around and up to make a large lower loop. Lay it across the intersection of the two loops as shown.

3. Wrap the cord behind the top loop to make a flat coil around the intersection of the two loops (see diagram 1).

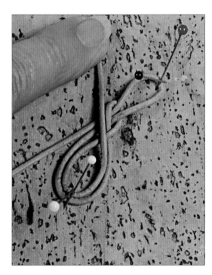

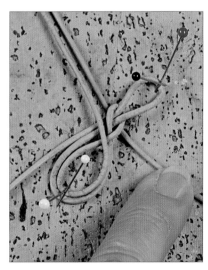

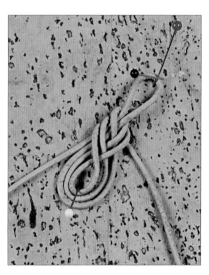

4. Bring the cord down, around and up again to make a smaller loop within the lower loop (see diagram 2).

5. Wrap it around and behind the intersection again, taking care that it curls inside and below the first coil.

6. Bring the cord down and around again to make a third loop inside the first two, then up again, around and behind to curl inside and below the previous coil.

7. Take the right-hand end and thread it through the centre of the lower loops (see diagram 3).

8. Take the left-hand end across the left side of the loops, over the newly threaded cord, then down through the hole in the centre and under the right side (see diagram 4).

9. Remove the knot from the cork mat, turn it over and secure the loose ends on the back with a dab of instant glue gel. Cut the excess cord off.

10. Thread the 50cm (20in) cord through the loop at the top, then thread a large bead sandwiched between two small beads on to the new cord.

11. Slide one of the earring hooks on to the new cord (see inset), then tie a button knot with one end of the new cord around the other. Move the hook and knot into place, then trim the excess cord.

12. Make a second earring in the same way to complete the pair.

Opposite

The necklace uses a single pipa knot as a decorative pendant, while the cord is made up of button knots in 1mm purple satin cord, interspersed with a mix of ceramic, glass and silver beads.

Both sets of earrings use ceramic and mixed glass beads to complement pipa knots made from leather cord.

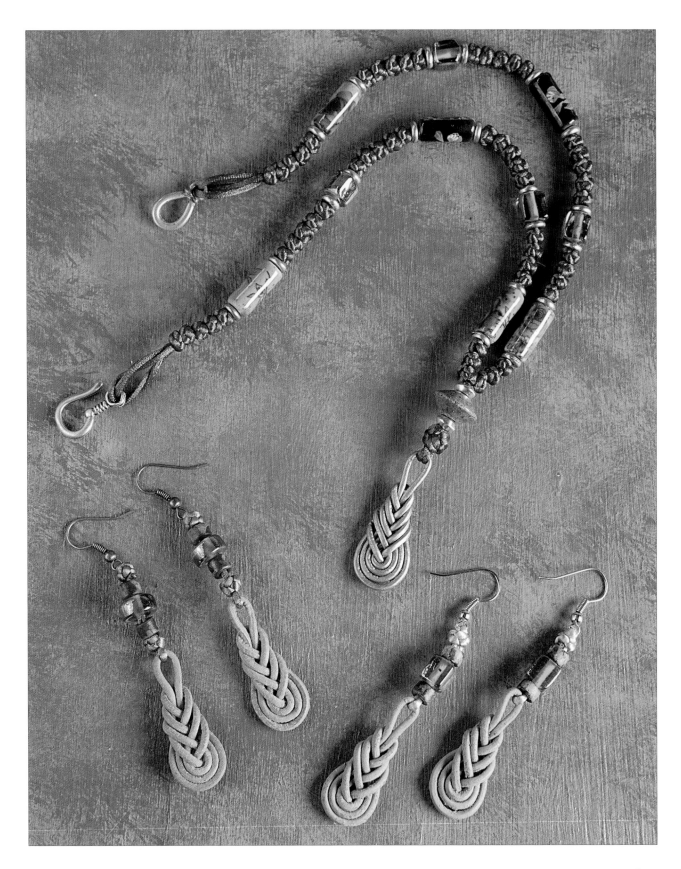

Square knot

Macramé necklace

This knot is known as a square knot in macramé, and the Chinese call it a flat knot. The ancient Egyptians and Greeks called it a Hercules knot, so it has a long and varied history.

In the 1970s macramé was very popular and mostly made with string and hemp. These days macramé is enjoying a revival, but since it is now generally made with much finer cords in vibrant colours, the finished pieces look much more sophisticated.

In parts of this necklace, only the first half of the square knot is tied repeatedly, and this causes the cords to twist, making a spiral knot. This knot is also very attractive, especially if the cord is shiny.

You will need

4.5m (177in) purple
1mm satin cord

1m (39in) purple 1mm satin cord

30cm (12in) purple 1mm satin cord

Silver-coloured toggle closure

Large flower bead (or similar large
decorative bead)

Five small white beads

One pearl bead

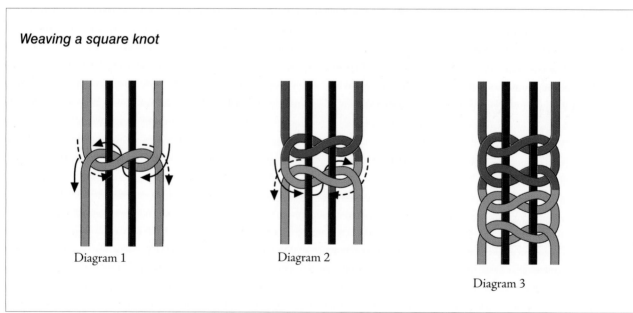

Weaving a square knot

Diagram 1

Diagram 2

Diagram 3

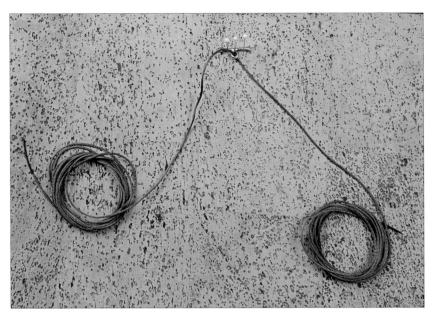

1. Slide the toggle closure up to the centre of the 4.5m (177in) purple cord and pin it to the board. These will be the knotting cords.

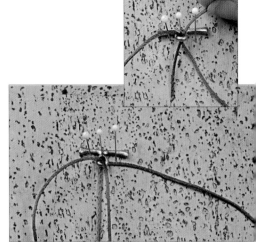

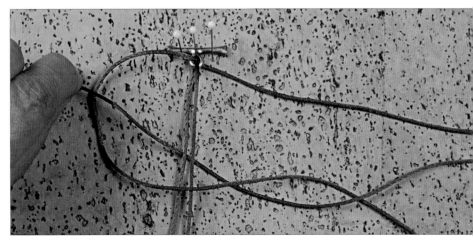

2. Slide the 1m (39in) purple cord through the toggle (see inset), then pull it through to the centre and run both ends down the board as shown. These are the 'lazy cords' (also known as 'core').

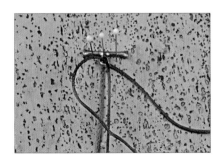

3. Take the left-hand knotting cord over the lazy cords, making a loop on the left.

4. Take the right-hand knotting cord over the left-hand knotting cord, under the lazy cords and up through the loop on the left.

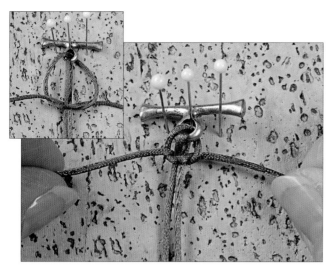

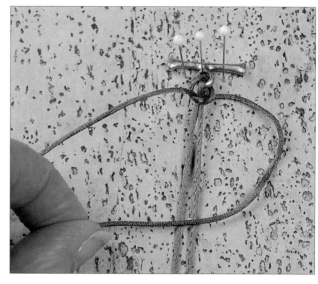

5. Pull the right-hand cord through (see inset), and tighten the knot (see diagram 1).

Note

This is the first half of the knot. If it is repeatedly tied, a spiral knot is made.

6. Take the cord on the right over the lazy cords, making a loop on the right.

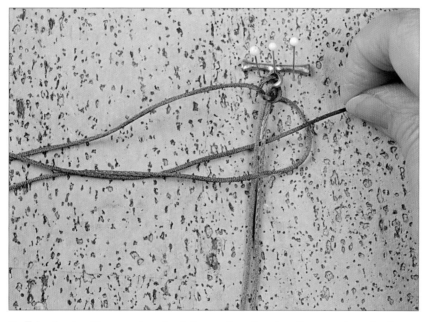

Tip

When making the square knot remember that the second cord goes 'over, under and up'. This will help you to build up a natural rhythm.

7. Take the knotting cord on the left over the other knotting cord, under the lazy cords and up through the loop as shown.

8. Pull the cord through the loop and tighten (see diagram 2). You have now completed one square knot.

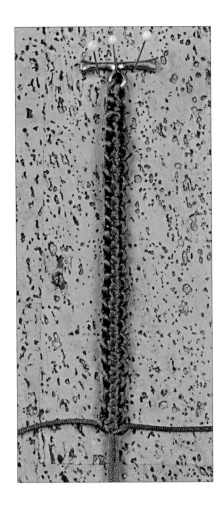

Note

The same knotting cord should always remain on top when you are making square knots.

9. Repeat the process from step 3 until the knots form a 12cm (4¾in) length.

10. Thread a white bead on to both lazy cords and run it up to the last square knot as shown.

11. This next section is made up of spiral knots, made in the following way: take the left-hand knotting cord over the lazy cords, making a loop.

12. Take the right-hand knotting cord over the knotting cord, under the lazy cords and up through the loop on the left.

13. Tighten the knot (see inset), then repeat from step 11 until the knots form a 7.5cm (3in) length. Note that if only the first half of the square knot (left over right) is repeated (rather than alternating left over right with right over left, as in the square knot), the knots will twist into a spiral. These are called spiral knots.

> **Tip**
>
> The tendency of spiral knots to twist is so strong that the work will spiral. Once you find the twist makes working difficult, simply turn the work over in the direction of the twist, pull the knotting cords round and continue.

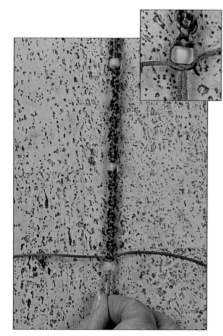

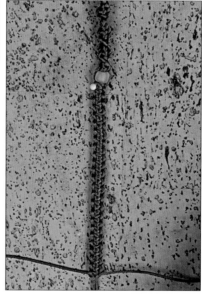

14. Secure a bead at the bottom of the spiral knots as before (see inset), then work another 7.5cm (3in) of spiral knots and thread on a third bead.

15. Secure the bead as before and work 12cm (4¾in) of square knots.

16. Unpin the work and place it on scrap paper with the working end at the top as shown. Thread the loop closure on to the lazy cords 1cm (½in) from the square knots.

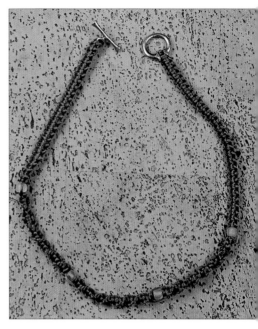

17. Fold the lazy cords over and cut them so that the ends reach the square knots (see inset), then glue the lazy cords down on themselves using instant glue gel.

18. When the glued cords are secure, pin the piece back on the cork board then work square knots over the glued piece as shown.

19. Trim and seal the ends to complete the basic necklace.

20. To make the pendant, set the necklace to one side, then make a button knot at one end of the 30cm (12in) cord. Thread on the two crystal beads and secure them in place with a second button knot.

21. Make a small overhand knot by taking the cord over itself 1cm (½in) above the button knot to hold the flower bead in place, then thread on the large flower bead.

22. Thread on the pearl bead, then take the end of the cord through the top of the flower bead so the bead sits in the centre of the flower. Pull the cord through and thread on the last small white bead.

Note

If it is not possible to find an identical large flower bead, substitute your own pendant for a different tassel. Do not worry: enjoy the creativity of making your own design!

173

23. Find the centre of the necklace and take the end of the pendant through as shown.

24. Take the end round and back through the small white bead.

25. Tie a button knot around the cord and move it up, then secure and trim to finish.

Opposite

The fantasy necklace at the top left uses seashells and pearls to complement the gold knotted cord. Below this are rings incorporating fused glass beads by Marlene Minhas. The blue, white and gold lampwork beads used on the blue necklace at the bottom are made by Rachelle Goldreich.

Four-leaved clover knot

Four-leaved clover necklace

Finding a four-leaved clover is considered to be very lucky both in China and the West. However if you can not find one, here is how to make one of your own! This knot is tied in a similar way to a clover leaf knot but with an extra leaf.

When it is finished it will need a couple of tiny drops of instant glue gel in the centre to hold it firmly, especially if it is made with satin cord.

You will need

One glass pendant

Two black beads and three decorative glass beads

60cm (24in) black 2mm satin cord

270cm (106in) black 2mm satin cord

270cm (106in) gold 2mm satin cord

A number of 30cm (12in) lengths of black 2mm satin cord

A number of 30cm (12in) lengths of gold 2mm satin cord

Fish and toggle closure

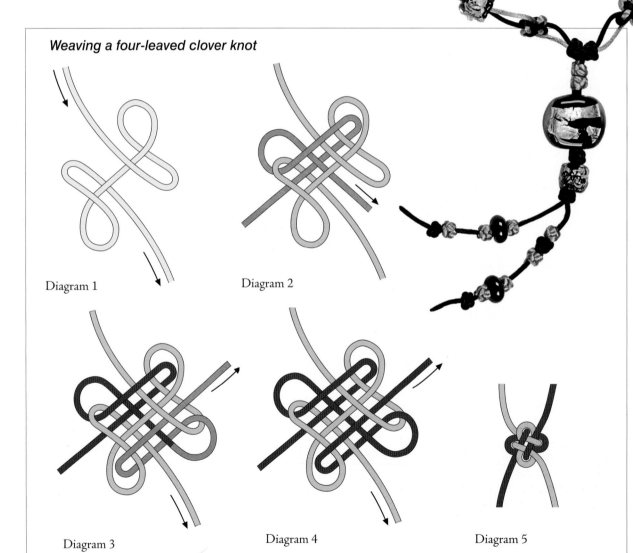

Weaving a four-leaved clover knot

Diagram 1

Diagram 2

Diagram 3

Diagram 4

Diagram 5

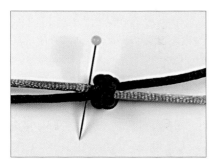

1. Lay the 270cm (106in) black and gold cords next to each other and place a pin through the centre of both cords to act as an anchor. Tie a button knot with the black cord around the gold cord and move it up to the pin (see page 14).

2. Remove the anchor pin and tie a second button knot with the other end of the black cord around the gold cord. Move it up next to the other knot.

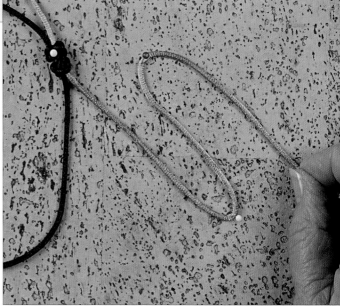

3. Pin the piece to the corkboard, then pin the gold cord into a wide 'S' shape as shown.

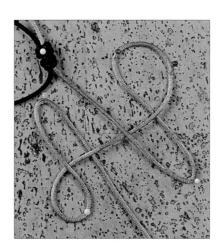

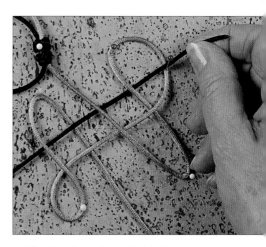

4. Take the end over then under the cord and draw through to make a loop at the top.

5. Pin the top loop, then make a second loop at the bottom. Pin and then make a doubled-back loop taking the end first over then under the cord as shown. See diagram 1.

6. Starting from the left side (as shown in diagram 2), take the black cord under the gold cord, over it, and then under twice and up through the loop at the top.

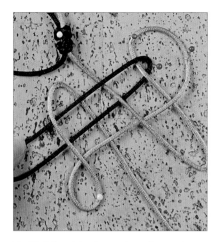

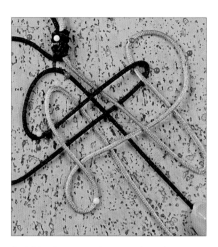

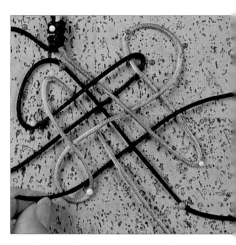

7. Pull the black cord up through the loop, then pin and weave it down over the first three cords and under the fourth.

8. Take it up and around to the right, then bring it down between the gold cords: under the first, over the second and under the third.

9. Take the black cord up to the right, then around to the left and down. Weave it over the first cord, under the next four and up through the gold loop.

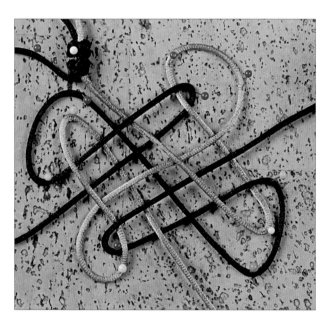

10. Take the black cord over two parts of the gold cord (see picture), over the black cord, under the gold cord and then over the last gold cord. Pull through to finish the weaving of the knot (see diagram 3).

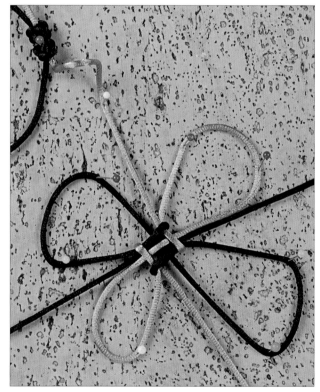

11. Begin to tighten the knot by removing pins and pulling the loose ends (as shown in diagram 4) until the centre of the knot is formed as shown.

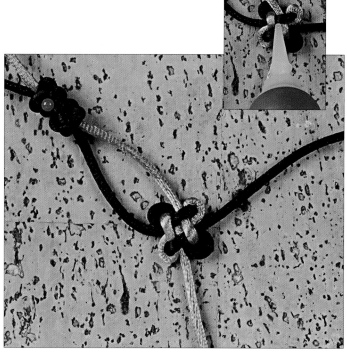

12. Continue to tighten the knot, being careful to ensure that the loops do not flip over out of place, as this will ruin the knot. They will flip over if not held down (see diagram 5).

13. Very carefully and gradually, move the knot up the gold cord towards the button knots and re-tighten 2cm (¾in) from the button knots. Add a dab of instant glue gel to secure the centre of the knot (see inset).

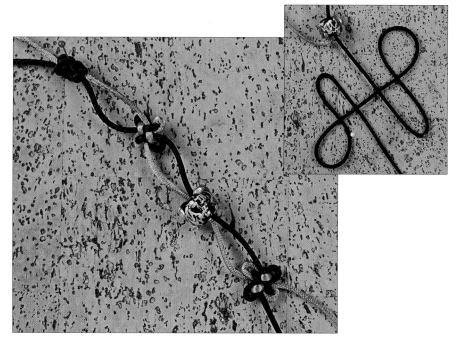

14. Thread a glass bead on to both cords, then tie a second four-leaved clover knot. Start with the black cord rather than the gold (see inset), and move it up to the bead, tightening it 2cm (¾in) below it.

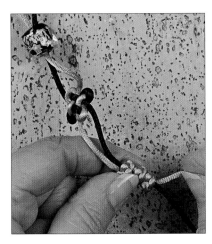

15. Leave a gap of 2cm (¾in), then tie three button knots around the black cord using the gold cord.

16. Tie three button knots around the gold cord using the black cord.

17. Slide the fish loop on to the cords and double the cords over. Tie a button knot with the gold cord around the three other cords to secure it in place.

18. Tie a black knot around the three other cords. Cut and seal the loose ends to complete the first half of the necklace. You have two sliding knots next to each other, making the finish less bulky than a double button knot using both cords.

19. Work the second half in the same way as the first, following steps 37, replacing the fish loop with a toggle.

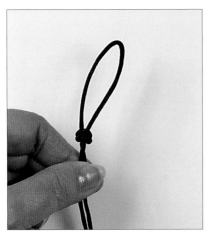

20. To make the pendant, take the 60cm (24in) black cord. Fold the cord slightly off-centre so that one end is approximately 5cm (2in) shorter than the other, and make a loop large enough to slip over the beads on the necklace and tie a button knot using one end of the cord around the other.

21. Slide the glass pendant over the loop down to the button knot, then use a pin to anchor it.

22. Slide a glass bead on to both free ends and slide it up to the button knots. Secure it in place with a second button knot.

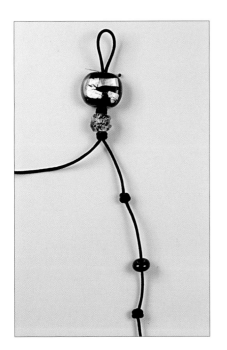

23. On the longer end of the cord, make a button knot 5cm (2in) down from the previous knot. Thread on a black bead, then tie another button knot near the end of the cord.

24. Thread a black bead on to the shorter end of the cord, then tie a button knot near the end of the cord.

181

Tip

These knots are tied on to the black cords in the same way as any other button knots, except that each has two loose ends to trim to make the knot.

25. Thread the pendant's loop on to the necklace so that it sits in the centre between the original black button knots (see step 2).

26. Use the short lengths of gold cord to tie as many button knots as necessary in the space between the button knots on the necklace and the large black and gold pendant bead.

The finished necklace.

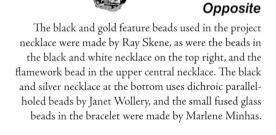

Opposite

The black and gold feature beads used in the project necklace were made by Ray Skene, as were the beads in the black and white necklace on the top right, and the flamework bead in the upper central necklace. The black and silver necklace at the bottom uses dichroic parallel-holed beads by Janet Wollery, and the small fused glass beads in the bracelet were made by Marlene Minhas.

182

Virtue knot

Dragonfly brooch

Dragonflies have long been admired for their delicate lacy wings, iridescent colour and fanciful, unpredictable flight. One legend has it that dragonflies are 'dragons' grandchildren' as they are believed to emerge from the cast-off skin of dragons. Chinese people believe that harming or trapping a dragonfly causes illness.

The knot is made from two cords tied as one to make a large button knot head, and a virtue knot to make the wings, then using the four cords a series of flat knots make the body. I like to leave a trailing tail but you can trim the cord at the end of the body if you prefer.

You will need

1.75m (69in) royal blue 1mm braided cord

1.75m (69in) turquoise 1mm braided cord

Brooch pin

Black leather

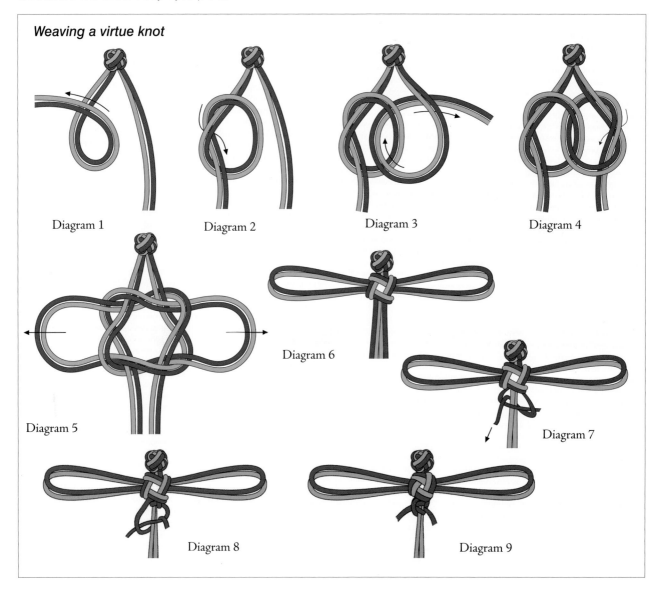

Weaving a virtue knot

Diagram 1

Diagram 2

Diagram 3

Diagram 4

Diagram 5

Diagram 6

Diagram 7

Diagram 8

Diagram 9

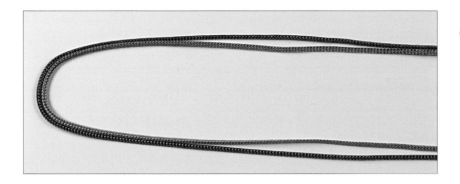

1. Lie both cords down alongside each other and find the centre.

2. Using the paired cords as one cord, tie a button knot by tying one pair of cords around the other pair and moving the knot to the centre.

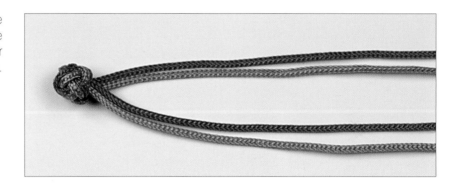

3. Place the piece on your corkboard and place a pin through the button knot. Take one cord of each colour to either side.

4. Using the cords on the left, make a loop as shown. Keep the cords parallel and do not let them cross over each other (see diagram 1).

5. Take the ends underneath and through the loop to make an overhand knot (see diagram 2).

185

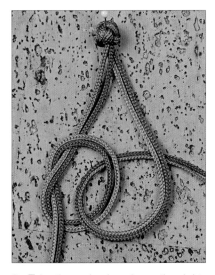

6. Take the paired ends on the right through the loop of the overhand knot, and then under itself to make a loop on the right (see diagram 3).

7. Take the ends underneath and through the loop to make a second overhand knot on the right.

8. The twists on the outsides of the loops make figures of eight (see diagram 4). Use a pair of tweezers to reach in through the top of the figure of eight on the left-hand side and grip the inside of the right-hand overhand knot as shown.

9. Carefully pull the gripped piece through the top of the figure of eight.

10. Repeat on the other side. Make sure that none of the cords have crossed over each other (see diagram 5).

186

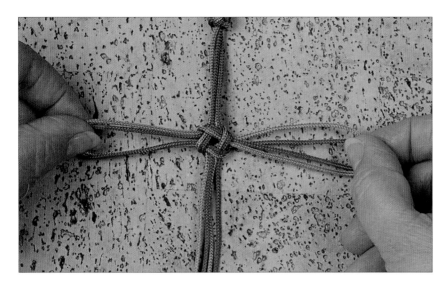

11. Carefully pull the loops out to form the virtue knot, but do not tighten it completely.

12. Ease the virtue knot up into position beneath the button knot to form the head and abdomen of the dragonfly.

13. Ease the cords through until the wingspan is roughly 8cm (3¼in). Tighten the knot to complete the virtue knot.

14. With the virtue knot in place, we will now make the square knot tail. Arrange the cords at the bottom as shown, with the turquoise as the knotting cords and the royal blue cords as the lazy cords.

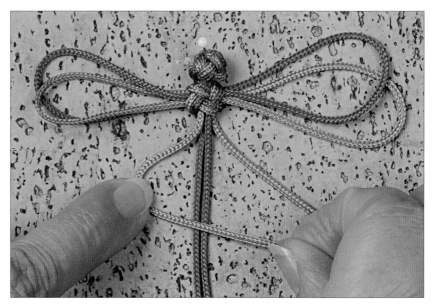

15. Take the left-hand knotting cord over the lazy cords to make a loop.

16. Take the left-hand knotting cord over the central lazy cords, then take the right-hand cord over the left-hand cord, under the lazy cords and up through the loop as shown.

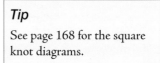

Tip
See page 168 for the square knot diagrams.

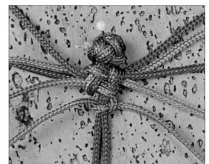

17. Gently tighten the knot so it sits underneath the abdomen.

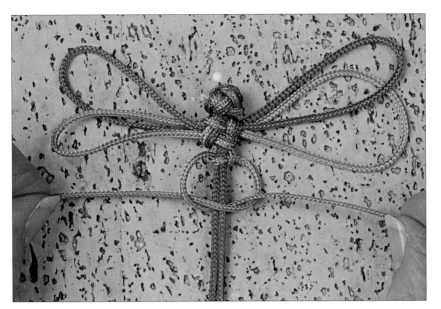

Tip

Remember that for square knots, the second cord goes 'over, under and up'; and that the same knotting cord should always remain on top.

18. Take the right-hand knotting cord over the lazy cords, then take the left-hand knotting cord over the right-hand knotting cord, under the lazy cords and up through the loop.

19. Tighten the knot to complete one square knot.

20. Gradually making the knots tighter (and hence smaller) as you continue, work square knots until the thorax is 7cm (3in) long.

21. Remove the anchor pin and trim and seal the turquoise cords. Trim and seal the royal blue cords to approximately 5cm (2in) as shown.

189

22. Secure a strip of leather to the back of the dragonfly with a little instant glue gel.

23. Once dry, glue the brooch pin back on to the leather.

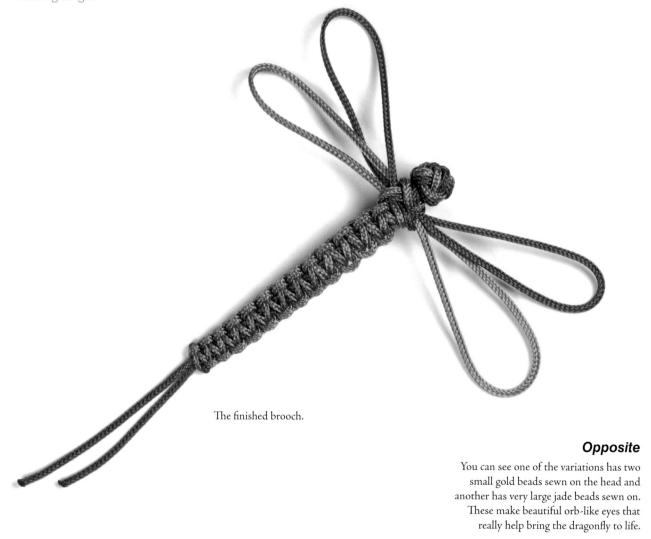

The finished brooch.

Opposite

You can see one of the variations has two small gold beads sewn on the head and another has very large jade beads sewn on. These make beautiful orb-like eyes that really help bring the dragonfly to life.

Index